POLAND

ABDO
Publishing Company

POLAND

by Christine Zuchora-Walske

Content Consultant
Padraic Kenney
Professor of History, Director of Polish Studies
Indiana University

CREDITS

Published by ABDO Publishing Company, PO Box 398166, Minneapolis, MN 55439. Copyright © 2013 by Abdo Consulting Group, Inc. International copyrights reserved in all countries. No part of this book may be reproduced in any form without written permission from the publisher. The Essential Library™ is a trademark and logo of ABDO Publishing Company.

Printed in the United States of America,
North Mankato, Minnesota
112012
012013

Editor: Rebecca Felix
Series Designer: Emily Love

About the Author: Christine Zuchora-Walske has been writing and editing books and articles for children, parents, and teachers for more than 20 years. Her author credits include books for children and young adults on science, history, and current events, as well as books for adults on pregnancy and parenting. Her book *Giant Octopuses* was an IRA Teacher's Choice book for 2001, and *Leaping Grasshoppers* was a 2001 NSTA/CBC Outstanding Science Trade Book for Students. Several of Zuchora-Walske's books have been well reviewed by *The Horn Book* and *School Library Journal.* She lives in Minneapolis, Minnesota, with her husband and two children.

Cataloging-in-Publication Data

Zuchora-Walske, Christine.
 Poland / Christine Zuchora-Walske.
   p. cm. -- (Countries of the world)
Includes bibliographical references and index.
ISBN 978-1-61783-634-3
1. Poland--Juvenile literature.   I. Title.
943.8--dc22

                                                    2012946082

Cover: Old Town in Poland's capital city of Warsaw

TABLE OF CONTENTS

CHAPTER 1
A VISIT TO POLAND

As your train crosses the border from the Czech Republic into Poland, you gaze out your window. Rolling green hills whiz by in the foreground. Occasionally you spot a cluster of cows, a quaint house, or a field of potato plants.

You flip through one of the tourist brochures you grabbed at the train station this morning. Its photos show the ski slopes, alpine meadows, snowcapped peaks, and charming wooden architecture in and around the town of Zakopane. You had no idea such a place existed in Poland. You hope you'll have time to visit there.

About an hour after crossing the border, you feel the train slowing down. The conductor announces the train is approaching the town of Oświęcim. When you hear the town's Polish name—which sounds much like its German name, Auschwitz—you get a chill. German Nazis killed more than 1 million people there during World War II (1939–1945).

Mount Giewont in the Tatra Mountains near the town of Zakopane

Seven decades later, the horrific reminders linger. The death camps aren't visible from the train station, but you know they're not far away. You can feel their presence.

The train makes its way east across the country, and now you're headed for Kraków, Poland. You have visited Prague in the Czech Republic and have heard many people compare it to Kraków. Now that you've seen the stunning beauty of Prague, you can't wait to experience its Polish counterpart.

A little under an hour later, your train approaches Kraków. You watch eagerly out your window. The city's outskirts do not impress you. All you can see are drab Soviet-style apartment blocks, the shabby backsides of homes and shops, and the occasional factory.

WORLD WAR II OCCUPATION AND OPPRESSION

In 1939, at the beginning of World War II, Nazis invaded Poland. The Nazi occupation lasted until 1945 and was the bloodiest, deadliest period in Poland's history. The Nazis placed severe restrictions on the Poles and enforced their rule cruelly. Poland became the main killing ground of the Nazi genocide. Nearly 6 million Polish citizens died during this time.[1]

At the end of World War II in 1945, the Soviet army liberated Poland from Nazi rule. The Soviet Union was a Communist federation including Russia and 14 other republics. It established a Communist government in Poland. Communism is a political-economic system that aims to distribute wealth equally among all people. Poland became a socialist state. In a socialist state, groups of workers or the nation itself—not individuals—own the nation's resources. Despite the government's stated intentions, life in Communist Poland was harsh. Ordinary people had a low standard of living and virtually no political freedom.

Political Boundaries of Poland

Finally, your train pulls into Kraków. You shoulder your big backpack and step down onto the platform. You stretch your legs with a walk to your hostel, 15 minutes away in Kraków's Old Town—or Stare Miasto, as the locals call it. It's too late to go sightseeing, so you turn in early.

The next morning, you wake up eager to take in Kraków's sights. There's so much to see! Kraków is one of the few cities in Poland that Nazi forces did not destroy. Evidence of Poland's long, dramatic history is rich here.

You decide to start at the Rynek Główny, also known as Market Square or Grand Square, at the center of Old Town. As you step out of a side street into the plaza, your jaw drops. It's huge! It's as big as ten football fields and lined with Renaissance-style town houses.

You head straight to the ornate building at the center of the square. This is the Sukiennice, or Cloth Hall. Merchants have been selling their wares from this site since the Middle Ages. You take your time inside the more than 700-year-old building, admiring the beautiful craftwork for sale. You buy a small, intricately carved wooden box as a memento and then head upstairs to the café. You choose a table outdoors on the terrace and order lunch.

As you eat, you hear a trumpet echoing across the square. The stirring sound is coming from the taller of the two towers atop Saint

The plaza at Old Town in Kraków is the largest medieval European plaza.

CENTRAL KRAKÓW

The entire center of Kraków is a United Nations Educational, Scientific and Cultural Organization (UNESCO) World Heritage Site. The site includes not only Rynek Główny and Wawel Hill, but the entire Stare Miasto—once surrounded by a medieval wall and moat that have been replaced by a green belt of parkland. It also extends to Kazimierz, the Jewish district south of Old Town. The site is home to dozens of churches, synagogues, university buildings, museums, monuments, sculptures, and gathering places that date back to the thirteenth century.

Mary's Basilica, where a bugler marks each hour of the day. The bugler suddenly halts mid-melody. You look around, puzzled. No one else seems to notice this oddity. You decide to head for Saint Mary's after lunch. You figure there must be a story behind the halting music.

You're right. As you tour the church, you learn it's almost as old as the Cloth Hall. You also hear a legend about how in ancient Kraków—as in many European cities—a bugle call signaled the opening and closing of the city's gates. In the thirteenth century, a guard in the church tower spotted Tatar soldiers from Asia approaching Kraków. He bugled to shut the gates but was shot in the throat by an arrow before he finished his tune. People heard the warning and fought off the invaders. Kraków's modern buglers reenact this legend every time they mark the hour.

A bugler plays on the hour from his perch in the tower of Saint Mary's.

Exiting the church, you walk along the edge of the square toward Grodzka Street. This wide avenue leads straight south to Wawel Hill. Wawel Hill is a limestone cliff overlooking the Wisła River, also known as the Vistula River, at the southern tip of Old Town. As you climb the hill, you feel like you're traveling back in time. Wawel is a very old place. Its stories, artifacts, and buildings date back to the seventh century. It is the birthplace of Poland, and for many centuries, it was also the capital. In fact, during the fifteenth and sixteenth centuries, it was the seat of Europe's largest kingdom, Poland-Lithuania. The sprawling complex includes a cathedral, castle, armory, residences, fortifications, gardens, tombs, caves, and ruins. You spend the rest of the day there, engrossed in the history of Poland.

POLAND-LITHUANIA

In 1385, Poland and its northern neighbor, Lithuania, joined forces. The kingdom of Poland-Lithuania became very large. It held together for more than four centuries. During this era, Poland experienced its golden age, a period of great prosperity and cultural achievement.

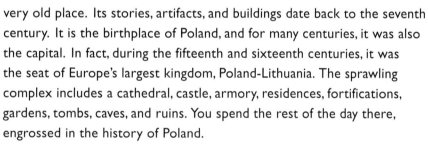

The Cathedral Basilica of Saints Stanisław and Wacław, more commonly known as Wawel Cathedral, sits on Wawel Hill in Kraków.

POLAND'S PARADOX

Walking back to your hostel, you think about all you've experienced during the past two days. In a very short time, you've passed through places that mark Poland's brightest and darkest days.

Warsaw is sometimes called "Phoenix City" due to its rebirth from almost complete destruction.

You're beginning to realize Poland is somewhat of a paradox. In this country, contradictory or contrasting things often stand side by side. Stunning beauty resides in buildings and historic sites that are next door to those containing remembrances of destruction and horror. Stories of oppression and death mingle with tales of survival and triumph. People who survived the bleak years of Nazi occupation coexist with youth too young to remember the Communist era that followed. To the people of Poland, the complexity is what makes the nation rich—and what makes it home.

SNAPSHOT

Official name: Republic of Poland (Polish: Rzeczpospolita Polska)

Capital city: Warsaw (Polish: Warszawa)

Form of government: republic

Title of leaders: prime minister (head of government); president (head of state)

Currency: złoty

Population (July 2012 est.): 38,415,284
World rank: 33

Size: 120,728 square miles (312,685 sq km)
World rank: 70

Language: Polish

Official religion (if any): none

Per capita GDP (2011, US dollars): $20,600
World rank: 60

CHAPTER 2

GEOGRAPHY: LAND OF PLAINS

Poland is largely a land of plains. In fact, that is essentially what its name means. *Poland* comes from the Polish word *pole*, which means "fields."

With the exception of mountains in the south, Poland's terrain is mainly low and flat. This terrain has strongly influenced Poland's history. The land is easy to travel across and farm, and its natural resources are relatively accessible. Poland contains few defensible geographic features, such as mountains and rivers, along its borders. As a result, Poland has been at the center of a nearly constant tug of war among powerful neighboring nations.

Poland's average elevation is 568 feet (173 m) above sea level.

A quiet river runs through one of Poland's many plains.

LOCATION AND SIZE

Poland lies in north-central Europe. The Baltic Sea forms Poland's northwestern edge. Germany is directly west, and the Czech Republic sits to the southwest. Poland shares its southern border with Slovakia. To the southeast lies Ukraine, and Belarus is directly east. Lithuania touches Poland's northeastern corner, and the Russian exclave of Kaliningrad shares Poland's northern border.

The total area of Poland is 120,728 square miles (312,685 sq km), which is just a little smaller than the US state of New Mexico. Within this area are five distinct geographic zones: mountains, uplands, central plains, the lakes region, and the Baltic coastal plain.

THE MOUNTAINS

Mount Rysy is 8,199 feet (2,499 m) tall.

Poland's highest, most rugged terrain is found along its southern border. Along the Czech-Slovak-Polish border lie a series of mountain chains, of which the Tatras are the highest. The Tatras are located at the western end of the great Carpathian Mountains. These mountains are part of a much larger range that arcs through the Czech Republic, Slovakia, Poland, Ukraine, Hungary, and Romania. Poland's highest peak, Mount Rysy, is in the Tatras, and it

Snow blankets the Tatra Mountains in the winter.

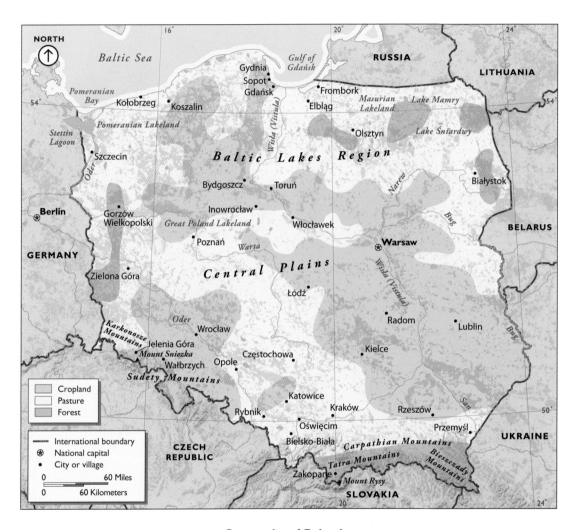

NORTH ↑

Baltic Sea

Pomeranian Bay

Gulf of Gdańsk

RUSSIA

LITHUANIA

Gydnia
Sopot
Gdańsk

Frombork
Elbląg

Masurian Lakeland

Lake Mamry

Kołobrzeg
Koszalin

Pomeranian Lakeland

Olsztyn

Lake Śniardwy

Stettin Lagoon

Szczecin

B a l t i c   L a k e s   R e g i o n

Wisła (Vistula)

Białystok

Bydgoszcz
Toruń

Berlin

Gorzów Wielkopolski

Inowrocław

Great Poland Lakeland

Włocławek

Narew

BELARUS

Poznań

Warta

Warsaw

Bug

GERMANY

C e n t r a l   P l a i n s

Zielona Góra

Łódź

Wisła (Vistula)

Oder

Radom

Lublin

Wrocław

Karkonosze Mountains

Jelenia Góra

Mount Sniezka

Wałbrzych

Opole

Częstochowa

Kielce

Bug

Sudety Mountains

Rybnik

Katowice

Kraków

Rzeszów

San

UKRAINE

Oświęcim

Przemyśl

Bielsko-Biała

Carpathian Mountains

Bieszczady Mountains

	Cropland
	Pasture
	Forest

Zakopane

Tatra Mountains

Mount Rysy

SLOVAKIA

——— International boundary
⊛ National capital
• City or village

0 ———————— 60 Miles
0 ———————— 60 Kilometers

CZECH REPUBLIC

Geography of Poland

straddles the Slovak-Polish border. One of Poland's two main rivers, the Wisła, begins in the Tatra Mountains. From there, it winds northward through eastern Poland in an S-shaped curve. It forms a wide delta as it approaches Gdańsk Bay on the Baltic Sea.

In the southwest, the Sudety Mountains cover the area where the borders of Poland, Germany, and the Czech Republic meet. The highest peak in this range, Mount Śnieżka, which is 5,256 feet (1, 602 m), straddles the Czech-Polish border in the Karkonosze Mountains. Poland's other main river, the Oder, begins in the Sudety Mountains. From there, it flows northward through western Poland, emptying into the Baltic Sea at Pomeranian Bay.

Compared to other mountain ranges in Europe, Poland's highlands are not particularly high. However, they are rugged and dramatic and, by all accounts, quite beautiful. Some of Poland's mountains are popular destinations for hikers, skiers, and mountain bikers.

Poland's mountains strongly affect the nearby climate. The wind usually

HALNY

The Tatra Mountains are known for the *halny*, a strong wind that blows there. The halny usually occurs in autumn but occasionally takes place in late winter. It develops when wind bumps into a mountain and is forced upward. That action causes rain on the windward side and warm, very high winds on the leeward, or downwind, side. The halny can snap trees, tear apart roofs, flatten fences, and cause sudden thawing, avalanches, and floods.

blows from the west in Poland, so the country's highest levels of precipitation fall on its mountains' western slopes. Snow covers the ground approximately 200 days of the year.[1] The Tatra Mountains have the highest precipitation in Poland. Temperatures in the mountains generally drop with rising altitude. Winter temperatures in mountain valleys may drop as low as minus 72 degrees Fahrenheit (-40°C).[2]

UPLANDS

Just north of the mountains lie the uplands. This region contains hills, low mountains, and plateaus. The uplands are approximately 56 miles (90 km) across in the west, widening to approximately 124 miles (200 km) in the east. The average altitude in the uplands is 656 to 984 feet (200 to 300 m). Its highest hills are approximately 2,008 feet (612 m).

In addition to coal, the uplands also hold deposits of iron ore, zinc, and lead.

The climate in the uplands is a bit warmer and drier than the mountain climate. July is the warmest month, and January is the coldest month.

The uplands are densely populated. Poland's richest farmland and much of its mineral wealth—including rich coal deposits—lie here. Kraków, Poland's second-largest city and most important cultural center, is found in the uplands.

Climate of Poland

Legend:
- Temperate, No Dry Season, Warm Summer
- Cold, No Dry Season, Warm Summer
- Cold, No Dry Season, Cold Summer
- Alpine Tundra

NORTH ↑

The plains and climate in central Poland are ideal for agriculture.

THE CENTRAL PLAINS

Poland's largest geographic zone lies north of the uplands. The *polesie*, or "central plains," are the country's defining feature. Similar to the uplands, the plains are narrower in the west and wider in the east. The terrain is mostly flat with the occasional gentle slope. It contains many rivers, streams, and ponds but no large lakes.

Land use in this region is mostly agricultural. The central plains are also home to four of Poland's five largest cities: Warsaw, which is the capital; Łódź, which is an industrial center; and Wrocław and Poznań, which are hubs for education and trade.

The climate of central Poland is continental. This means it has warm, moderate summers and cold, snowy winters. As in other areas, the warmest month in central Poland is July, and the coldest month is January. Central Poland is drier than both the mountains and the uplands, with approximately 188 days with precipitation each year.[3]

AVERAGE TEMPERATURE AND PRECIPITATION

Region (City)	Average January Temperature Minimum/Maximum	Average July Temperature Minimum/Maximum	Average Precipitation January/July
Mountains (Zakopane)	12/19°F (-11/-7°C)	41/51°F (5/11°C)	4.6/8.1 inches (11.7/20.6 cm)
Lesser Poland uplands (Rzeszów)	21/30°F (-6/-1°C)	54/73°F (12/23°C)	0.8/3.4 inches (2.0/8.6 cm)
Central plains (Warsaw)	24/33°F (-4/1°C)	55/73°F (13/23°C)	1.1/3.0inches (2.8/7.6 cm)
Lakes region (Olsztyn)	21/30°F (-6/-1°C)	54/71°F (12/22°C)	1.3/5.2 inches (3.3/13.2 cm)
Baltic coastal plain (Gdańsk)	28/35°F (-2/2°C)	56/72°F (13/22°C)	1.4/2.8 inches (3.6/7.1 cm)[4]

THE LAKES REGION

The lakes region lies north of Poland's central plains. This region is known for its low hills, which formed during prehistoric times. Receding glaciers melted, filling depressions with water and leaving behind large mounds of debris. Wide, shallow river valleys divide the lakes region into three main parts: the Pomeranian Lake District in the west, the Great Poland Lake District in the center, and the Masurian Lake District in the east.

LAND OF LAKES

Most of Poland's lakes that are larger than 2.5 acres (1 ha) lie within Poland's lakes region. Poland is home to 9,300 lakes. Finland is the only European nation with a higher density of lakes than Poland.

The soil in the lakes region is sandy or marshy, and therefore it is not ideal for farming. However, the region is perfect for nature tourism. The region includes Europe's only remaining primeval forests. Many canals connect the lakes and rivers to one another, as well as to the Baltic Sea, forming an extensive system of waterways. These waterways—and the hills and forests surrounding them—attract outdoor enthusiasts of all kinds, including canoeists, anglers, campers, hikers, and bikers.

Small islands rise from one of Masuria's many lakes.

The climate is cooler overall in the lakes region than the rest of Poland. Winter arrives in the Masurian Lake District first before creeping southward and westward. Its lakes are usually frozen from December through April. Spring is wet, while summer is generally dry.

The Baltic Sea is the world's second-biggest brackish body of water, containing a mixture of salt water and freshwater.

THE BALTIC COASTAL PLAIN

The Baltic coastal plain is Poland's northernmost geographic zone. This region is a strip of lowlands lining Poland's entire Baltic shore. It stretches approximately 273 miles (440 km) from Pomeranian Bay on the Polish-German border to near its border with Kaliningrad.

The entire region is low and flat. Its landscapes include seaside dunes and cliffs, river deltas, lagoons, and bogs. An area of approximately 23 square miles (60 sq km) along the Gulf of Gdańsk lies below sea level.

The Baltic coastal plain is home to two important seaports. Szczecin lies near the mouth of the Oder River, which empties into Szczecin Lagoon and the Pomeranian Bay. Gdańsk is a seaport and a key industrial city found near the mouth of the Wisła River, which empties into Gdańsk Bay. Gdańsk, along with the nearby city of Gdynia and the resort town of Sopot, make up a large metropolitan area known as Trójmiasto, or Tri-City.

This region has an oceanic climate. Proximity to the sea prevents extremes in cold or heat. The sea also brings rain to the region, making it almost as wet as the mountains.

SOPOT

Nestled between the industrial giants of Gdynia and Gdańsk is the resort town of Sopot. Sopot was settled in the thirteenth century. It has been a spa town since the sixteenth century, and its first public baths were built in the nineteenth century. Its shopping, cuisine, nightlife, and beaches draw tourists from all over Europe. Sopot is best known among Poles for its *molo*, or "pier," which is the longest wooden pier in Europe. It is also home to the Krzywy Domek, or "Crooked House." This extremely odd-shaped structure was inspired by the work of Polish illustrator Jan Marcin Szancer.

CHAPTER 3

ANIMALS AND NATURE: PROGRESS AND PRESERVATION

Poland is home to a rich variety of plant and animal species. This biological diversity stems from several causes. For example, many types of terrain exist at different altitudes across the country. Oceanic and continental air masses meet over Poland, providing distinct seasons with various kinds of weather. Poland has no natural barriers on the west or east, which makes it easy for plant and animal species to migrate.

POLAND'S ANIMALS

Approximately 33,000 species of animals live in Poland.[1] The Baltic coastal plains and the lakes region are home to many kinds of birds and mammals.

White-tailed eagles, Poland's national bird, hunt fish by hovering over water and then striking the prey with their sharp talons.

Topping this list is Poland's national bird, the white-tailed eagle. This eagle has a beige head and neck, a dark brown back, wings, and belly, and a white tail. It is Poland's largest bird of prey, with a wingspan of eight feet (2.5 m). The white-tailed eagle lives in the Baltic coastal plain, where it hunts fish and waterfowl. This European eagle was once gravely endangered, but conservation efforts starting in the 1970s have helped the population thrive again.

The white-tailed eagle is also called the sea eagle.

The Biebrza wetlands in northeastern Poland provide a resting place and breeding ground for hundreds of species of waterfowl, birds of prey, and other birds. In spring and autumn, when many birds are migrating, the flapping, fluttering, honking, quacking, screeching, chirping, and splashing of thousands of birds can be heard from miles away. The lakes region hosts elk, dear, beavers, otters, and a wide variety of smaller mammals.

The Baltic Sea is a mixture of freshwater from rivers and salt water from the Atlantic Ocean. Its low salinity and stillness make it a poor habitat for most marine animals. The Baltic Sea's fauna include small clams and shrimplike crustaceans. The most common fish are cod, herring, hake, plaice, flounder, shorthorn sculpin, and turbot. Seals and porpoises appear occasionally along Poland's coast. Poland's large rivers are too polluted to support much wildlife. However, its smaller rivers and lakes teem with tench, carp, perch, pike, eel, bream, trout, whitefish, powan, burbot, and thunderfish.

On the plains of Poland live different communities of animals. Humans have altered the natural habitat with many farms and cities, but not so much that it has killed or driven out all animals. Mice, voles, hamsters, and partridges thrive in Polish farm fields. Sparrows, swifts, swallows, pigeons, and turtledoves populate rural and urban buildings. A complex of old concrete tunnels in west-central Poland is home to thousands of bats. In the eastern plains live mammals, such as the steppe polecat, which is a type of weasel, and the spotted souslik, which is a type of squirrel. There are also many types of birds, including owls, snipes, and cranes. Several

ENDANGERED SPECIES IN POLAND

According to the International Union for Conservation of Nature (IUCN), Poland is home to the following numbers of species that are categorized by the organization as Critically Endangered, Endangered, or Vulnerable:

Mammals	5
Birds	6
Reptiles	0
Amphibians	0
Fishes	7
Mollusks	6
Other Invertebrates	15
Plants	11
Total	50[2]

BIAŁOWIEŻA BISON

The herd of bison that live in the Białowieża Forest are European bison, a large breed that can grow as tall as six feet (1.8 m) and as long as nine feet (2.7 m). They live in Poland, Lithuania, Belarus, the Russian Federation, Ukraine, and Slovakia. Wild European bison were on the brink of extinction in the eighteenth century. Two small herds—one in Poland and one in the Caucasus, which is a mountainous region stretching from southern Russia to northern Iran—survived through the nineteenth century. However, people killed the last members of both herds early in the twentieth century. Only a few European bison remained in zoos and closed preserves. To save the species, Polish scientists established a captive breeding program in the Białowieża Forest in 1929. Since then, the population has steadily increased to approximately 800 in 2009.[3] The forest's managers have transported many bison to other European forests as well to help the species recover more of its original range.

hundred European bison— Poland's biggest mammal— roam the Białowieża Forest in this area.

Poland's uplands and mountains provide homes for several large mammals, such as brown bears, deer, wolves, lynx and other wildcats, and chamois, which are wild goat-antelopes. Smaller mammals include foxes, badgers, and marmots. The mountains contain many birds of prey, such as eagles, owls, buzzards, and peregrine falcons. There are also carrion birds, such as kites, and ground birds, including capercaillies and grouse.

Chamois graze on a rocky hillside in the Tatras Mountains.

UNIQUE PLANTS AND MANY FORESTS

Poland has the greatest diversity of plants in central Europe. In the Baltic coastal plain, conditions are perfect for plants that thrive in a cool, wet environment. The cross-leaved heath, for example, is an evergreen shrub with pink bell-shaped flowers. It grows profusely along Poland's seacoast, as well as in its wetlands. Poland's coast is also home to many kinds of trees. Among these are the Swedish whitebeam, a deciduous tree with bright red berries. Poland's coast is the southern boundary of this tree's range. Beautiful beech forests grow near the cities of Szczecin in the northeast and Elbląg on the northern coast.

Poland is home to 4,750 different plant species.

The lakes region of Poland is bursting with unique communities of plant life. The region's web of lakes, rivers, and wetlands support plants that thrive in unpolluted water and wet, acidic soil. For example, the Pomeranian Lake District is home to more than 100 lobelia lakes. These lakes earn their name from the rare water lobelia flowers that grow in them. Water lobelia have spongy leaves growing beneath the water and small white flowers rising on slender stalks above the surface. These flowers grow only in clean, still lakes with acidic water rich in carbon dioxide. Poland's lakes region also contains vast untouched marshlands and peat swamps. Its thick forests are made up mostly of evergreens, such as spruce trees, but oaks, hornbeams, beeches, birches, and alders are also found there. Mosses, ferns, and berry bushes grow on the forest floor.

Water lobelias are called *lobelia jeziorna* in Polish, or "lobelia lake."

Water lobelias are called *lobelia jeziorna* in Polish, or "lobelia lake."

The central plains of Poland are more sparsely forested. Outside the cities and towns, this area contains mostly farmland and grassland. Where the soil is too poor for farming, people plant pine trees for lumber, shade, and protection from wind and erosion. In the far eastern plains, however, lies a precious tract of forest. The Białowieża Forest straddles the Poland-Belarus border. It is the last remaining stand of the primeval lowland forest that once covered most of Europe. It is a mixed forest consisting of towering spruces, a canopy of oaks, lindens, and maples, and an understory of ash trees. Approximately 3,000 species of fungi also live here.[4] They grow on the decaying remains of ancient trees.

Poland's uplands are thick with forests. These forests contain many kinds of trees, but firs and yews are especially common. Many of Poland's yews are more than 600 years old. The biggest and oldest yews measure more than 16 feet (5 m) around. Rare wildflowers, including several species of orchids, violet marsh gentians, and yellow globe flowers, as well as large patches of raspberries and blackberries, grow in these forests.

Poland's most extensive forests are in the mountains. Larch, spruce, fir, and beech trees grow in abundance in the mountain region. A variety of flowers grow only there. These include saxifrages, which are low-growing rosettes with succulent leaves, chrysanthemums, violets, and many others. The Tatra and

A yew tree growing near the city of Jelenia Góra in southwestern Poland is nearly 1,300 years old.

Old-growth trees are plentiful in Białowieża Forest.

Bieszczady Mountains are home to spectacular meadows. These vast, high meadows are covered with grasses and bilberry bushes. In spring, they burst into bloom with thousands of crocuses.

PROTECTED LANDS

The Polish people have developed their land unevenly and sporadically, leaving portions of varying habitats intact. Poles also farm mostly on a small scale, which disrupts the natural environment less than industrial agriculture does. However, Poland has had severe problems with pollution from mining, manufacturing, and coal-fired power plants. This pollution has caused some of Poland's ecosystems to disappear. The nation has had to find ways to make the most of its natural resources without destroying them.

One way Poles have preserved critical habitats is by setting aside national parks. Designation as a national park grants protection for all of nature within the park's borders. Poland currently has 23 national parks scattered throughout the country, and the government is in the process of establishing

BARTEK OAK TREE

Bartek is a famous oak tree found near the city of Kielce, in southern Poland. The tree is approximately 700 years old. It stands 98 feet (30 m) tall and measures 44 feet (13 m) around. According to legend, this tree has long been a favorite of Poland's leaders. Several historic kings are said to have camped and held court around it, prayed under it, and hidden weapons inside it.

three more in eastern Poland.[5] The country has a long history of protecting valuable tracts of natural land. The Białowieża Forest, for example, has been a protected area for half a millennium. Approximately five centuries ago, Polish kings set aside the forest for hunting, and they banned people from logging and living there. People have largely left the forest alone since then. In 1932, it became Poland's first national park, Białowieża National Park. In 1979, UNESCO designated it a World Heritage site.

Another key site is Biebrzański National Park. This park is Poland's largest at 229 square miles (593 sq km). It protects the Biebrza River wetlands in northeastern Poland. Biebrzański National Park protects a large, diverse community of plants, mammals, fish, and birds that is unique in Europe. It is considered a wetland of international importance.

ENVIRONMENTAL CHALLENGES

When Poland emerged from Communist rule in 1989, the environment was damaged. Four decades of neglect and abuse had taken a terrible toll. The air, water, and soil were severely polluted with waste from mining, manufacturing, and coal-fired power plants. The river water was undrinkable and could not be used for irrigation. Acid rain created from air pollution had damaged approximately two-thirds of Poland's forests and one-half of its lakes. Conditions were especially bad in the densely populated and industrialized uplands, which was apparent in public health statistics. The rates of infant mortality, circulatory and respiratory disease, lead content in children's blood, and cancer were higher in the

EUTROPHICATION

More than one-quarter of the Baltic Sea is a dead zone, especially near Poland and Germany, where it receives significant agricultural runoff. When large quantities of farm fertilizer collect in a body of water, the nutrients encourage rapid growth of microscopic, free-floating aquatic plants such as algae. This process is called eutrophication. It reduces the amount of oxygen available for other plants and animals. In addition, some algae, such as the blue-green algae observed in the Baltic Sea, produce chemicals that are poisonous to humans.

uplands than in other parts of Poland, and they were much higher than in Western Europe.

Poland's economy was dependent for a long time on industries that pollute the environment, so the nation had to change its ways gradually. Throughout the 1990s, Poland worked steadily to clean up its environment and transform its economy.

When Poland joined the European Union (EU) in 2004, it agreed to adopt a new and challenging set of environmental policies. As a result of these policies, Poland's air, water, and soil quality have improved dramatically. However, Poland still struggles with air pollution and acid rain caused by its coal-fired power plants, as well as water pollution from urban areas and industry.

After years of damage from industrial pollution, Poland now strives to protect its unique natural environments.

CHAPTER 4

HISTORY: POLAND'S PERSEVERANCE

The Polish people can trace their country's Polish history back more than 1,000 years. For thousands of years before that, Poland was home to a wide variety of peoples and cultures. Since the time of its earliest inhabitants, Poland has persevered through a full range of human drama— from peace and prosperity to war and disaster.

ANCIENT POLAND

Historians have found no written records of Poland's earliest history. However, they have found archaeological artifacts that offer clues about life in prehistoric Poland.

The oldest archaeological evidence of humans in this area dates to approximately 800,000 BCE. Poland's Stone Age lasted from

Archaeologists have found many ancient artifacts in Poland, such as this horse sculpture created between 4000 and 3000 BCE.

approximately 800,000 to 2,300 BCE. For most of this time, the climate was very cold. People lived mainly in southern Poland. They moved from place to place as they hunted animals and gathered plants for food. They made tools of stone to help carry out their daily activities. In the mountain village of Kończyce Wielkie in southern Poland, scientists have found remnants of these stone tools, made by the area's earliest human inhabitants.

In approximately 5,500 BCE, a wave of immigrants spread across Europe. These people lived in settled communities. They kept livestock and farmed the land. They hunted, fished, and gathered plants off the local lands. They made tools out of pottery and stone. Eventually, settled farming societies dominated Poland. By approximately 2,300 BCE, people were making tools of metal—first bronze and then iron. The period of time from approximately 2,300 to 650 BCE was called the Bronze Age, followed by the Iron Age, which took place from approximately 650 BCE to 500 CE.

During the late Bronze Age and early Iron Age, the Lusatian culture prevailed in Poland. Many people belonging to this culture lived in fortified settlements. They farmed, kept livestock, hoarded valuable weapons and jewelry, and cremated their dead. They built forts on sites with natural defenses, such as islands, peninsulas, or high ground surrounded by marshes. They constructed protective barriers around their villages by filling wooden boxes with soil or stones. Biskupin, built in the 730s BCE and since restored, is one famous Lusatian settlement. It lies near Żnin.

A depiction of a Polish village
during the Iron Age

During Poland's late Iron Age, neighboring civilizations had a dramatic impact on Poland. The Celts, an Indo-European ethnic group with their own Celtic religion and language, lived to the west of Poland. Another Indo-European ethnic group, the Germanic people, who spoke Germanic languages and followed their own religion, lived in what is now northern Poland. Both societies' religions were complex, and both groups possessed excellent metalworking skills. Their people and practices steadily infiltrated Poland.

The Roman Empire lay to the south of Poland. Romans considered the residents of Poland to be uncivilized savages, but they still traded extensively with them. Amber from the shores of the Baltic Sea was a key trade product.

MEDIEVAL POLAND

Around 500 CE, another great wave of migration began. The Roman Empire was crumbling. Germanic people in Poland moved south into former Roman lands. Meanwhile, a group of people called Slavs, an ethnic group hailing from the east, moved into Poland.

The Slavs formed many small tribal domains ruled by noblemen. None of the tribes were very powerful. The early Slavs followed pagan religions. They revered the forces and phenomena of nature. The most widely worshiped Slavic god was the all-seeing Świętowit. He is depicted with four faces, holding a cornucopia in his right hand and a sword in his left hand. Other well-known deities are Dziewanna, goddess of spring; Lada, goddess of order and beauty; Marzanna, goddess of death; Perun, god of storms; Radegast, the protector of merchants and guests; and Welles, god of cattle. The Slavs believed nymphs, sirens, and fauns filled the woods and waters.

Early Slavic religion included the belief in an after world, and funerals were very elaborate.

In 962, Otto I became emperor of the Holy Roman Empire, a large, powerful Christian realm with the kingdom of Germany at its heart. Otto wanted to expand his empire eastward, so he attacked his Slavic neighbors, including those in the area of current-day Poland.

Among the Slavic tribes in medieval Poland were the Polans, Vistulans, Czechs, and Moravians. At this time, Mieszko I was leader of the Polans. He became king in 963. Under Mieszko, the Polans subdued the other Slavic tribes in Poland, eventually forming a kingdom that stretched from the Baltic Sea to the Carpathians. Once united, the Slavs could better defend themselves against Otto's armies. Mieszko converted himself and his people to Christianity in 966. Most historians recognize this event as the birth of the state of Poland. Mieszko's conversion to Christianity prevented Otto's efforts to gain support from other Christians by claiming God was on his side. It thwarted an attack by the Holy Roman Empire.

Mieszko I was the first king of Poland.

PIAST

Polish legend says Piast was a peasant who lived in the ninth century CE. His neighbor, Prince Popiel, turned away two uninvited travelers from a feast he was hosting. The travelers called upon Piast next. Piast welcomed the strangers into his humble home—along with the stingy Popiel and all of Popiel's guests—and invited everyone to join his son's birthday feast. In return for this hospitality, the strangers performed a miracle. No matter how much food or drink Piast served, it never ran out. The locals saw this as a prophecy about the Piast family. They made Piast their leader. Eventually, his offspring ruled all of Poland. Mieszko was Piast's great-great grandson.

Mieszko died in 992. Over the next several generations, the Piast dynasty, Mieszko's descendants, expanded and strengthened the kingdom of Poland. In 1138, the kingdom was divided among five heirs to the throne. Fighting ensued among church leaders, wealthy people, and the five rulers, weakening Poland's defenses.

In the thirteenth century, Poland suffered a series of destructive invasions from the Tatars, a nomadic ethnic group from central Asia that spoke Turkic languages. Meanwhile, a Polish duke invited the Teutonic Knights, an organization of German Christian military crusaders, to help him conquer pagan tribes along the southeastern shores of the Baltic Sea. The knights did so but then turned on the Poles who had invited them in by conquering Polish lands. By 1300, most of Poland was occupied by foreigners.

Poland regained its footing during the fourteenth century, beginning a centuries-long period of strength and stability. King Władysław I won back enough territory through strategic alliances to win acceptance as king of Poland—not just a fragment of Poland. His son, Kazimierz III, was a wise administrator and diplomat. He founded the University of Kraków, today known as the Jagiełłonian University, in 1364, turning the city into a key cultural center. During Kazimierz's reign, the Black Death, a pandemic infection, swept across Europe, killing millions. But Poland established quarantines at its borders, and the plague skirted Poland almost entirely. Kazimierz welcomed into Poland thousands of Jews who were being blamed for the plague and persecuted elsewhere in Europe.

By the late fourteenth century, Kazimierz's grandniece, Jadwiga, had become queen of Poland. In 1385, she married Jagiełło, the ruler of Lithuania, a pagan realm that Poland had struggled with over religion, land, and cultural issues during the previous century. At this time, the two kingdoms put aside their past quarrels and joined forces in the Union of Krewo. This union marked the end of the Piast dynasty and the beginning of the Jagiełłonian dynasty. United, Poland and Lithuania fared better against their common enemies, including the Mongols, Tatars, and German Teutonic Knights. Jagiełło agreed to convert to Christianity along with his people. He changed his name to Władysław II and became king of Poland-Lithuania. He ruled for nearly 50 years.

King Kazimierz III became known as Kazimierz the Great.

Poland-Lithuania included much of modern Poland and Lithuania, as well as parts of modern neighboring nations. During the next century, its territory continued expanding and growing in power. By 1500, Poland-Lithuania covered almost all of central and eastern Europe.

THE GOLDEN AGE AND ITS COLLAPSE

Historians consider the 1500s to be the golden age of Poland. During this time, Poland-Lithuania experienced great prosperity and cultural achievement.

Farms were the foundation of the kingdom's wealth. Western Europe's population was booming, and Poland-Lithuania was its breadbasket, or main source of food. The grain trade filled the kingdom's treasury, enriched its landowners, and encouraged Poland's society to remain mostly rural while cities mushroomed across the rest of Europe.

Poland-Lithuania differed from the rest of Europe in another way. Elsewhere, money and power flowed toward royalty. But in Poland-Lithuania, the aristocracy kept a great deal of wealth and control. It organized a parliament called the Sejm, whose approval was necessary to pass all laws.

During the sixteenth century, the Protestant Reformation occurred. The Roman Catholic Church, which had dominated Europe until this time, was splitting into two factions. Bloody wars between the two Christian groups—the Catholics and Protestants—troubled much of Europe.

But Poland continued its custom of religious tolerance. Protestants in the strongly Catholic nation were persecuted at first, but the Sejm stopped it. In 1552, the Sejm outlawed death sentences for the religious crime of heresy, or contradicting Catholic beliefs. In 1573, it passed the Warsaw Confederation, which guaranteed freedom of religious practice for all.

Also during the sixteenth century, the Renaissance came to Poland. The Renaissance was a cultural movement that started in Italy and spread slowly across the rest of Europe. Its process was accelerated in Poland-Lithuania by the marriage of then-king of Poland Zygmunt I, a descendent of the Jagiełłonian dynasty, to Italian noblewoman Bona Sforza. This period saw Polish art, architecture, literature, music, science, and education bloom. The University of Kraków became an internationally respected intellectual center, and its most famous student, Nicolaus Copernicus, revolutionized the science of astronomy. The Polish Renaissance continued under King Zygmunt II, who became ruler after his father Zygmunt I's death in 1548.

NICOLAUS COPERNICUS

Nicolaus Copernicus (Mikołaj Kopernik in Polish) was born in Torun, Poland, in 1473. In 1491, he enrolled at the University of Kraków. There, he discovered a passion for mathematics and astronomy. He chose a career in the Catholic Church, but he used every spare moment to study the night sky. His observations led him to a shocking conclusion: he believed Earth and the other visible planets orbited the sun, and that Earth was not the center of the universe. This idea contradicted church teachings and the opinions of most scholars, but it turned out to be true.

When Zygmunt II died in 1572, the hereditary monarchy—and the Jagiełłonian dynasty—ended. After this, Poland-Lithuania started declining. Its monarchy grew weak, and the Sejm gained great power. The Sejm's rules called for unanimity in decision making, which was nearly impossible to achieve. The government had difficulty getting things done. The kingdom found itself in constant territorial conflicts with Sweden, Russia, and the Ottoman Empire. The Ottoman Empire was a Muslim realm based in the city of Constantinople, which is now Istanbul, Turkey. Poor leadership, trouble with neighbors, and another plague epidemic sapped Poland-Lithuania's money and energy throughout the seventeenth century.

Many European nations considered Poland-Lithuania's third partition an international crime, but none opposed.

Meanwhile, Prussia, Austria, and Russia grew very powerful. Prussia was a large German kingdom that spanned across central Europe. Beginning in 1772, these three powers carved up Poland-Lithuania three times. After the third partition in 1795, Poland-Lithuania disappeared from the map of Europe.

Polish nationalists mounted a series of armed rebellions through the nineteenth century, mostly against Russia. But their attempts failed, and the nation of Poland remained invisible on the European map for more than a century, divided under the rule of three empires. Polish intellectuals and artists, such as poet Adam Mickiewicz, composer Frédéric Chopin, and novelist Henryk Sienkiewicz, however, kept Polish culture and identity alive throughout Poland's long absence.

The first partition of Poland in 1772 was followed by a second in 1793 and a third in 1795.

THE WORLD WARS

In 1914, World War I (1914–1918) broke out in Europe. Serbia provoked hostilities with the empire of Austria-Hungary. Previous treaties soon brought the German Empire, which included Prussia, and other nations to Austria-Hungary's aid. This group was called the Central powers. Likewise, Russia, Great Britain, France, and other nations joined Serbia. This group was called the Allied powers. Both sides promised Poles future self-rule and other concessions in return for loyalty and military service.

Poland was a key battleground during World War I. Two million Polish soldiers fought with the armies of Prussia and Austria and for opposing Russian armies.[1] More than 1 million Poles died—approximately half were soldiers, and the other half were civilians.[2] When Russia retreated from Poland and the Central powers collapsed at the end of the war, Poland reappeared on the map of Europe.

Although World War I was over, Poland and Russia continued to fight with each other. Russia was now a Communist country called the Soviet Union. Its army invaded Poland, hoping to install a Communist government there. But at the Battle of Warsaw in 1920, Marshal Józef Piłsudski led Polish forces to a surprising victory.

The people of Poland promptly established a democratic government. The new government faced a tough task. It had to repair extensive war damage, rebuild Poland's economy, and reintegrate Poland's divided people and territory into one nation. The new government proved unable to maintain political control or prevent an economic crisis.

In 1926, Piłsudski took control of Poland in a military coup. For the next decade, he held Poland together as a benevolent dictator. Although he answered to no one but himself, he generally used his power for the good of Poland. His main foreign policy goal was to keep Poland's still-strong neighbors, Germany and the Soviet Union, at bay. He tried to avoid relying on—or angering—either country. He signed nonaggression

Marshal Józef Piłsudski in Warsaw in 1927

pacts with both of them. This strategy failed. The German and Soviet leaders were far more ambitious than Piłsudski.

Then, in 1933, Adolf Hitler rose to power in Germany, and his Nazi Party established control over the government. Hitler intended to take over Europe and purge it of ethnic groups he deemed undesirable, lesser members of the human race. In 1939, Poland refused to give up the Baltic coast to Germany. Meanwhile, the Nazis and the Soviets secretly signed a nonaggression pact. Then Germany attacked the city of Gdańsk on Poland's Baltic coast, starting World War II. A few weeks later, the Soviet army attacked from the east. Poland could not withstand a double attack by two strong armies. Within a month, Poland fell. Germany occupied western Poland, and the Soviet Union occupied eastern Poland. By June 1941, Germany pushed out the Soviet Union and occupied all of Poland.

These were Poland's darkest days. Poland became a central battleground of World War II and the main killing zone of the Holocaust. Before the Soviets left, they deported approximately 1.7 million Poles to labor camps or exile to the steppes or other barren land in the Soviet Union.[3] The Nazis herded Polish Jews into walled-off ghettos in the main cities, where tens of thousands died of starvation, disease, brutality, and murder. The Nazis also built concentration camps and death camps, where prisoners were detained, tortured, and killed, all over Poland. Nazi Germany's largest concentration camp, Auschwitz, was in the city of Oświęcim.

Children at Auschwitz in Oświęcim in January 1945

By the end of the war, approximately 15 percent of Poles were dead.[4] This toll included nearly all of Poland's 3 million Jews, plus a similar number of Christian Poles.[5] Warsaw and many other cities and towns were destroyed.

Despite these horrors, Poles resisted Nazi Germany stubbornly. Poland was the only country to fight Nazi Germany from the first day of the war to the last in 1945. Tens of thousands of Poles who escaped their homeland fought against Germany and its partners, known as the Axis nations, with the Allied nations, including the United States. Within Poland, the Home Army and Jewish resistance groups fought against Nazi rule using sabotage, spying, and a series of armed uprisings.

From July 1944 to March 1945, the Soviet army gradually freed Poland from the Nazis. The Soviet Union had joined the Allies after Germany attacked the Soviet Union and broke the nonaggression pact between the two countries in 1941. Leaders of the main Allied nations—the United States, the United Kingdom, and the Soviet Union—agreed to place Poland within the Soviet sphere of influence, which was an area in Europe where Soviets had significant influence on culture, economy, and politics. The Allies eventually defeated the Axis nations, and the war ended in Europe on May 8, 1945. The Allied powers redrew Poland's borders to their current locations, giving Poland some German land and giving the Soviet Union some Polish land.

POLAND TODAY

Although the war had ended, oppression continued in Poland. With strong support from the Soviet Union, Communists won control of the postwar Polish government. This government rebuilt Poland's war-ravaged infrastructure and economy, but it did so at great cost to Polish society. The government outlawed noncommunist political parties, imprisoned opposition leaders, persecuted church members, and took over all industries. Poles found they could not express their opinions freely and had difficulty getting the consumer goods they needed.

From the mid-1940s to the mid-1970s, Poland's economy grew under Communist rule, but so did its people's discontent. When the economy began faltering in the late 1970s, Poles began opposing their government more openly. In 1980, shipyard workers in Gdańsk went on strike, demanding better civil rights, labor reform, and the right to establish a trade union free of Communist control. The workers refused to back down and eventually got what they wanted in the Gdańsk Agreement. Thus, the Solidarity trade union was born. It grew rapidly. Before long, 25 percent of Poles, or approximately 10 million people, had joined.[6] Solidarity became the main vehicle for opposing Communist rule.

From 1981 to 1983, Communist authorities imposed military law to strengthen their failing grip on Poland. The army and special police units seized control of the country, arrested Solidarity leaders, and outlawed union activity. But union members kept operating secretly—even in jail. Throughout the 1980s, Poland's economy continued deteriorating. More and more Poles believed communism had failed them.

By the late 1980s, Poland's Communist leaders realized their days in power

LECH WAŁĘSA AND KAROL WOJTYŁA

Poland's anticommunist movement succeeded largely because of two charismatic, determined men: Lech Wałęsa and Karol Wojtyła. Wałęsa was the leader of Solidarity. He won the Nobel Peace Prize in 1983 for his "determination to solve his country's problems . . . without resorting to violence."[7] Wojtyła was a cardinal in the Polish Catholic Church until his election as pope in 1978. As Pope John Paul II, he encouraged Poles to stand up for their rights. Wałęsa credited the pope for the fall of communism in Europe. He said, "The pope started this chain of events that led to the end of communism. . . . He simply said: 'Don't be afraid, change the image of this land.'"[8]

were numbered. They held talks with the leaders of Solidarity and other opposition groups. These talks led to an agreement allowing Solidarity to run candidates in the 1989 parliamentary election. In the June election, Communist candidates lost all the seats they had to contest in the senate. However, in the Sejm, Communists were granted 173 seats to Solidarity's 161 seats.[9] In August, a new Solidarity-led government began replacing the Communist system with a democracy and free-market economy.

In the 1990s, Poland made steady progress toward these political and economic goals. Since 1991, all Polish elections have been free and fair. Transfers of power have been peaceful and orderly, and parties upholding social equality have controlled both the parliament and presidency. In 1999, Poland joined the North Atlantic Treaty Organization (NATO), a military alliance of mainly North American and European countries. It joined the EU in 2004.

In 2010, Poland's president, Lech Kaczyński, and many other senior government and military officials died in a plane crash. This accident had the potential to create chaos in Poland. Instead, the Polish people came together to mourn their loss and rebuild their government peacefully.

Lech Wałęsa was Polish president from 1990 to 1995 and the leader of the Solidarity movement.

CHAPTER 5
PEOPLE: SHARED ROOTS

Poland has a long history of religious and ethnic tolerance. Because of its openness, unhindered geography, partition among empires, and lack of a strong state, Poland had a diverse population before World War II. In 1931, Poland's nationalities included ethnic Poles as well as large numbers of Ukrainians, Ashkenazi Jews, Belarusians, Germans, Russians, and Lithuanians. Its people practiced Catholicism, Orthodox Christianity, Judaism, and Protestant Christianity.

World War II dramatically changed Poland's demographics. The Holocaust devastated the Jewish population of Poland. Most Germans left or were forced to leave Poland at the end of the war. The postwar map of

Poland is the thirty-third most populous nation in the world.

A group of Poles make an annual religious pilgrimage to Częstochowa each August. A large majority of Poland's people are Catholic and ethnic Poles.

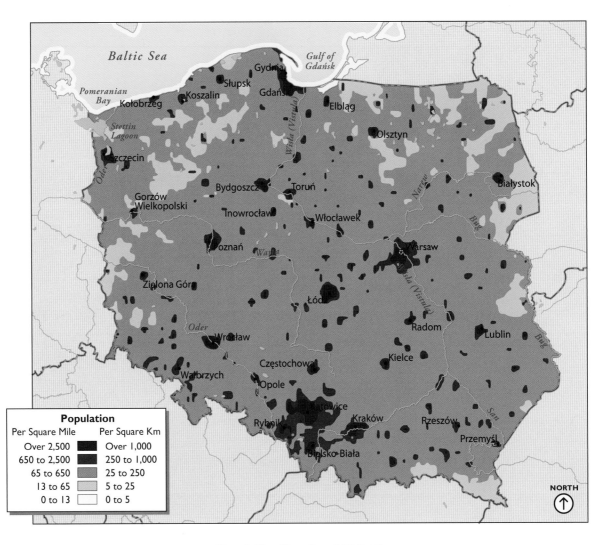

Population

Per Square Mile		Per Square Km
Over 2,500		Over 1,000
650 to 2,500		250 to 1,000
65 to 650		25 to 250
13 to 65		5 to 25
0 to 13		0 to 5

NORTH

Baltic Sea

Gulf of Gdańsk

Pomeranian Bay

Stettin Lagoon

Gydnia
Słupsk
Koszalin
Gdańsk
Kołobrzeg
Elbląg
Szczecin
Olsztyn
Gorzów Wielkopolski
Bydgoszcz
Toruń
Białystok
Inowrocław
Włocławek
Poznań
Warsaw
Zielona Góra
Łódź
Oder
Radom
Lublin
Wrocław
Kielce
Wałbrzych
Częstochowa
Opole
Katowice
Rybnik
Kraków
Rzeszów
Przemyśl
Bielsko-Biała

Wisła (Vistula)
Narew
Bug
Warta
Wisła (Vistula)
San

Population Density of Poland

Europe placed the majority of Poland's Ukrainians, Belarusians, Russians, and Lithuanians within the Soviet Union. As such, some of them were also forced to leave. In 1931, approximately two-thirds of Poland's people were Roman Catholic Poles.[1] Today, almost the entire population matches that description.[2]

POLAND'S DEMOGRAPHICS

Today, Poland is home to approximately 38 million people. Poland's birth and death rates are nearly equal, so the country's population is neither growing nor shrinking. Ethnic Poles make up 96.7 percent of the population. Germans

THE ROMA IN POLAND

Europe is home to millions of Roma, a people whose ancestors migrated to Europe from India approximately 1,000 years ago. In modern times, the Roma still speak Romani, a family of languages closely related to the Indian languages Hindi and Urdu. The Roma are one of Poland's smallest ethnic groups, numbering 20,000 to 30,000 members.[3]

The Roma in Poland belong to two main subgroups with differing dialects and customs. The Carpathian Roma historically lived settled lives in southern Poland. They were mainly blacksmiths and musicians living on the outskirts of villages. After World War II, most Carpathian Roma moved to cities. The Polish Roma historically lived nomadic lives and worked as horse traders, blacksmiths, fortune-tellers, and musicians. Since 1964, they have been forced to settle in communities.

Many Roma people live in poverty on the fringes of society. They often suffer discrimination from mainstream society. However, this problem is not as severe in Poland as it is in other European countries.

compose 0.4 percent. Belarusians and Ukrainians each account for 0.1 percent. The remaining 2.7 percent of Poland's people belong to other ethnic groups, including Roma.[4]

More than two-thirds of Poles are 15 to 64 years old. The rest of the population is divided fairly evenly between children and elders. Life expectancy is approximately 76 years. Women tend to live a few years longer than men in Poland.[5]

Poland has long been a rural, agricultural nation. Approximately 73 percent of Poles lived in rural areas in 1931.[6] But as its economy became more industrial under communism, Poland's population balance shifted. Today, 61 percent of Poles live in cities, while 39 percent live in rural areas.[7]

LANGUAGE

Polish emerged as a distinct language in the 900s CE— around the time the kingdom of Poland emerged.

Poland's official language is Polish. It belongs to the West Slavic family of languages and is closely related to the Czech and Slovak languages. Poles, Czechs, and Slovaks can usually understand one another without an interpreter. Foreigners often find Polish difficult to learn and speak. It has complicated grammar rules, and its consonant-heavy words are hard for foreigners to pronounce. For example, *chrząszcz*, the Polish word for "beetle," has one vowel sandwiched among eight consonants!

YOU SAY IT!

English	Polish
Hello/Good day	dzień dobry (djen DOH-bree)
Good-bye	Do widzenia (doh vee-DZEN-yah)
Good evening	Dobry wieczór (DOH-bree VYEH-choor)
Good night	Dobranoc (doh-BRAH-nohts)
Please/You're welcome	proszę (PROH-sheh)
Thank you	dziękuję (djen-KOO-yeh)
Yes	Tak (tahk)
No	Nie (nyeh)
How are you?	Jak się masz? (YAHK sheh mahsh)

Approximately 98 percent of Poland's residents speak Polish as their first language.[8] In addition to Polish, 14 other languages are spoken in Poland. The most widely used of these secondary languages are German, Belarusian, and Ukrainian.[9]

RELIGION

Religion has been an important part of Poland's nationhood since Mieszko adopted Christianity and formed the kingdom of Poland in 966 CE. World War II dramatically changed Poland's ethnic makeup and transformed the nation's religious profile. Roman Catholicism had long been the dominant religion before the war. At that time, approximately 60 percent of Poles were Roman Catholic. However, other religions were still prevalent. For example, approximately 30 percent practiced a variety of other Christian religions, and approximately 10 percent were Jewish.[10] After the war, Roman Catholicism essentially took over in Polish society. Today, 89.8 percent of Poles are Roman Catholic, 8.6 percent are unspecified, 1.3 percent practice Eastern Orthodox Christianity, 0.3 percent are Protestant, and nearly none are Jewish.[11]

The Roman Catholic Church is the world's largest Christian denomination.

Roman Catholicism plays a very important role in Polish society. During the time of the partitions, the Nazi occupation of Poland, and the Communist era, while other social networks were eliminated, repressed, or reorganized, churches grew stronger. They served as moral and ethical guides; provided encouragement, consolation, and a

A congregation attends mass in a Roman Catholic church in Kraków. Faith is pervasive in many aspects of life and highly valued by the majority of Poles.

sense of community; preserved Polish culture; and became the framework upon which Poles could organize a movement to overthrow their oppressors. Roman Catholicism continues to be a key element of Polish

THE *BLACK MADONNA*

Polish Catholicism focuses strongly on Mary, the mother of Jesus. Many shrines dedicated to Mary are scattered throughout the country. The most important of these is the shrine of the *Black Madonna* at the Jasna Góra monastery in Częstochowa. The *Black Madonna* is an ancient painting of Mary and the Christ Child that has darkened with soot and age. This portrait is credited with many miracles, and it attracts pilgrims from around the world. Saint Luke the Evangelist, one of the writers of the gospels, is said to have painted the *Black Madonna*. In fact, legend says he "painted a portrait of the Virgin on the cedar wood table at which she had taken her meals."[13] The portrait changed hands throughout the centuries, making its way from Jerusalem to Constantinople to Europe.

culture today. Most Poles who identify themselves as Catholics regularly attend church, and Catholic beliefs influence Polish politics.

The Eastern Orthodox Church, officially named the Orthodox Catholic Church, is the world's third-largest Christian denomination.[12] Like Roman Catholicism, the Eastern Orthodox Church is an international church. Unlike Catholicism, Orthodox Christianity does not have a single leader. Bishops are the leaders of Orthodox Christian communities, and each bishop has the final word over his community. Orthodox churches are generally organized by nation, such as the Polish Orthodox Church.

One religious leader earned the respect of most Poles, regardless of religion. If you ask everyone, "Who's the most famous Pole you can think of?" chances are good you'll hear one man mentioned repeatedly: Karol Wojtyła. Wojtyła, better known as Pope John Paul II, presided over the Roman Catholic Church from 1978 to 2005. He was one of Poland's most productive and widely read writers. Pope John Paul II studied literature intensively, spoke 12 languages, and published dozens of works. His influence extended beyond the Catholic Church to people of all backgrounds in every corner of the world.

Although Pope John Paul II was an international leader, he was also a symbol of Polish culture. His life, like Poland's history, is a story of spiritual strength and triumph against great odds. Pope John Paul II came of age in a dangerous and severely restricted Poland—first the Nazi occupation and then the Communist era. In addition to surviving the war, he secretly attended seminary during the war. He served many years as a priest under an atheist government, helping Poles

GREEK CATHOLICISM

Greek Catholicism is a branch of Christianity that emerged in the sixteenth century. In 1596, the Orthodox and Roman Catholic churches of Poland-Lithuania entered into a communion, or spiritual relationship, in which both denominations recognize they share essential principles and doctrines. The communion created conflict between those who did and did not accept it. Not all Orthodox parishes among Ukranians in Poland followed this communion. But centuries later, many had become Greek Catholics.

call upon their faith and unique identity to sustain them. Pope John Paul II went on to become a revolutionary pope, both encouraging the faithful and reaching out in friendship to diverse peoples.

Pope John Paul II published 16 nonfiction books, three books of poetry, seven plays, and other works.

Pope John Paul II in Zakopane, Poland, in 1997

CHAPTER 6
CULTURE: PROUDLY POLISH

Poland has produced scores of celebrated writers, including five who have won the Nobel Prize in Literature. All five focused on the spirit, people, and history of Poland in their writing.

Henryk Sienkiewicz (1846–1916) is remembered as "the patriot novelist of Poland."[1] He lived his entire life during the era of partitions and published several epic historical novels about Poland. In telling the stories of these times, he tried to help his fellow Poles preserve their identity and encourage them to keep struggling for freedom. In 1905, Sienkiewicz won a Nobel Prize for his lifetime achievements as a writer.

Another Nobel Prize–winning author living during this time was short-story writer and novelist Władysław Reymont (1867–1925). Reymont drafted works portraying the everyday lives of Poland's people.

A bookseller in Kraków stands proudly among his wares, which include the works of Poland's many celebrated and prize-winning authors.

He won the Nobel Prize in 1924 for his four-volume epic novel *Chłopi* (*The Peasants*).

Alive for nearly the entire twentieth century, Isaac Bashevis Singer (1902–1991) was born into a devout Polish-Jewish family. He immigrated to the United States in 1935, where he wrote many novels, short stories, and children's books. Most of Singer's work is set in Poland, written in Yiddish, and rich with folk tales. Singer won the Nobel Prize in 1978 "for his impassioned narrative art which, with roots in a Polish-Jewish cultural tradition, brings universal human conditions to life."[2]

Czesław Miłosz (1911–2004) began writing poetry during the 1930s. He worked in the Polish Resistance during World War II, and he left Communist Poland in 1951. Settling in the United States, he published an autobiographical novel, a book of essays, and many poems examining his own—and his country's—troubles. He won the Nobel Prize in 1980.

The fifth Polish author to win a Nobel Prize was Wisława Szymborska (1923–2012). Szymborska lived her entire life in Poland. After surviving the Nazi occupation, she supported communism at first. Later, she spoke out for freedom in her poems. She was known for her

WISŁAWA SZYMBORSKA

Wisława Szymborska was known as "the Mozart of poetry."[3] She was also known as the "guardian spirit" of Poland.[4] Her reputation rested on a relatively small number of poems—fewer than 350. When asked why she published so few poems during her life, Szymborska replied, "I have a trash can in my home."[5]

understatement, irony, and humor. She published more than a dozen books of poetry and won the Nobel Prize in 1996.

FILM

Cinema came to Poland soon after its invention in 1889. Poland's first cinema opened in Łódź in 1899. Half a century later, the world-renowned Łódź Film School opened. Since then, the school has produced numerous acclaimed actors, directors, photographers, and other cinematic professionals.

Films in Poland were censored during Communist rule in the 1980s.

A group of screenplay writers and film directors who called themselves the Polish Film School was active from the mid-1950s to the mid-1960s. They focused on the complexity of life in wartime and postwar Poland. The group is still intact today, and its most celebrated member is Andrzej Wajda. He explores the idea of Polish heroism in many of his dozens of films. He made his first film in 1955 and continues to direct films today. He has received countless awards for his work, including an honorary Oscar in 2000 for his contribution to world cinema.

Krzysztof Kieślowski began his training as a teenager in the late 1950s. He made several documentaries and feature films in the 1970s and 1980s, but he is better known for his later work. The 1990 film *The Double Life of Veronique* portrays two women living parallel lives. The Three Colors Trilogy: *Blue*, *White*, and *Red*, released in 1993 and 1994,

Roman Polanski on a 2001 film set in Warsaw

explores the virtues symbolized by the French flag: liberty, equality, and fraternity.

Among the many notable Polish filmmakers, Roman Polanski is perhaps the most famous. Polanski attended the Łódź Film School in the 1950s and began directing films in the 1960s. His many credits include the critically acclaimed *Knife in the Water* (1962), *Rosemary's Baby* (1968),

Chinatown (1974), *Tess* (1979), *The Pianist* (2002), and *The Ghost Writer* (2010).

MUSIC AND DANCE

Poles can trace their musical history back to the tenth century CE, when their forebears converted to Christianity. The conversion brought to Poland a new world of sacred music. From then on, much of Poland's early music honored Mary and other saints.

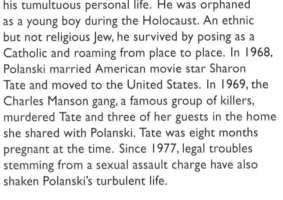

POLANSKI'S TUMULTUOUS LIFE

Roman Polanski is famous for his work as well as his tumultuous personal life. He was orphaned as a young boy during the Holocaust. An ethnic but not religious Jew, he survived by posing as a Catholic and roaming from place to place. In 1968, Polanski married American movie star Sharon Tate and moved to the United States. In 1969, the Charles Manson gang, a famous group of killers, murdered Tate and three of her guests in the home she shared with Polanski. Tate was eight months pregnant at the time. Since 1977, legal troubles stemming from a sexual assault charge have also shaken Polanski's turbulent life.

During Poland's golden age in the sixteenth and seventeenth centuries, both religious and secular music thrived. Poland's royal court, the aristocracy, and the church employed musicians from all across Europe. These musicians developed choral music, court dances, and a wide variety of songs.

Then, in the eighteenth century, Polish musical life suffered during Poland's decline. But after Poland disappeared from the European map

While many music genres are popular and important to contemporary Poles, several classical composers, including Krzysztof Penderecki, influence today's music culture.

in 1795, music became a way to assert the Polish cultural identity. During this time, Polish pianist and composer Fryderyk Szopen, better known as Frédéric Chopin (1810–1849), became a national hero for the stateless Poles. Chopin developed a distinct Polish style in classical music. His works incorporated elements of Polish folk music and dance, such as the triple-time mazurka and polonaise. Chopin's legacy influenced many composers and virtuoso performers of the late nineteenth and early twentieth centuries.

In the mid-twentieth century, a more modern, avant-garde style of Polish classical music took shape. Henryk Górecki (1933–2010) composed orchestral works known for their romantic harmonies and melodies in minimalist forms. Krzysztof Penderecki (1933–) has composed a huge repertoire of choral, symphonic, operatic, and chamber music. He is famous for writing ambitious religious works despite Communist disapproval. Many of his compositions have been adapted for film sound tracks.

Contemporary Polish pop music embraces a wide variety of genres, from jazz to punk and blues to heavy metal. Hip-hop is particularly important in Poland. Styles from Western Europe and North America strongly influence Polish pop music. Poland hosts many music festivals every year, each attracting tens of thousands of visitors.

Polish folk dancing is alive and well in Poland—especially in the mountainous southern region. Polish ballet combines elements of folk dances, classical ballet, and modern dance.

> **The earliest written Polish hymn is "Bogurodzica" (Mother of God) from the thirteenth century.**

ARTS, CRAFTS, AND ARCHITECTURE

Polish visual art was influenced by all the major movements that occurred throughout Europe, from the Romanesque style in the Middle Ages to modern art. One of Poland's most important art movements was the historicist school. It was developed in Kraków by Jan Matejko (1838–1893). Living during the days of partitions, Matejko wanted to show Poles their history. To do so, he painted scenes from Poland's past in dramatic and accurate detail. By the end of his life, Matejko had created several hundred oil paintings and thousands of drawings. Many

Poles are familiar with Matejko's work, having studied it alongside their history lessons in school.

Among Poland's many folk arts, *wycinanki*, or paper cutting, is the best known. Polish peasants traditionally decorated their homes with stenciled or hand-painted designs. When colorful paper became widely available in the nineteenth century, Poles began using these designs to create intricate paper cuttings. They typically hung the wycinanki from roof beams or along the tops of walls. The practice faded as Poland became more urban in the twentieth century. However, because the Communist regime valued Poland's native art forms, it preserved and promoted wycinanki.

DESTRUCTION AND CONSTRUCTION

Polish cities suffered heavy damage during World War II. Fighting damaged some cities, such as Gdańsk, Wrocław, and Szczecin. The Germans deliberately destroyed others, such as Warsaw. In these cities, architecture that seems ancient often is not. The postwar government meticulously rebuilt old neighborhoods to emphasize Poland's will to survive. Some areas, however, remained largely untouched by Nazi forces. Kraków is one example. Modern Kraków is home to many historic buildings that actually are as old as they look.

Like Polish art, Polish architecture reflects Poland's millennium-long history. It spans a wide range of styles, from the Romanesque and Gothic churches of medieval Poland to the ornate buildings of the Renaissance, the neoclassical mansions of the seventeenth and eighteenth centuries, and the modernist architecture of the 1930s. Poland's urban areas contain many good examples of socialist realist architecture built after World War II, such as the skyscraper Palace of Culture and Science in Warsaw, built in the 1950s. Urban areas were planned to accommodate the influx of workers caused by industrialization. They have wide streets, large public spaces, and vast stretches of stark apartment buildings. Central areas are devoted to government buildings, and factories are generally on the outskirts of town. This type of architecture and urban planning exists throughout Poland, except in Kraków, which retains much of its ancient structure.

Kraków's Sukiennice (Cloth Hall) is an example of Renaissance architecture.

CUISINE

Polish cuisine shares many traits with the food of other Central European countries. It includes a great deal of meat; cool-weather vegetables, such as potatoes, beets, carrots, cabbage, and legumes; and dairy products, such as milk, sour cream, buttermilk, whey, cheese, and butter. Bread, eggs, and various types of noodles are common foods as well. Well-known and popular dishes in Poland include kielbasa, a type of sausage; pierogi, or filled dumplings; and poppy-seed pastries and cakes.

Poles typically eat four meals per day. A large early breakfast of eggs, meat, cheese, and bread and jam occurs between five and eight o'clock in the morning. Between nine and eleven o'clock, many Poles eat a second, smaller breakfast similar to an American bag lunch. Dinner is the day's main meal. Poles eat dinner between one and five o'clock

Pierogi are a Polish staple and are traditionally stuffed with potatoes or meat.

in the afternoon. It usually includes a bowl of soup, a main dish that is sometimes accompanied by a salad, and a dessert. The day's last meal is a light supper eaten between six and eight o'clock in the evening. Supper is often a repeat of the first breakfast, but with more of an emphasis on meat than bread.

Poles commonly serve tea and coffee after meals. Many Poles consider tea an everyday beverage, reserving coffee for special occasions.

HOLIDAYS

Nearly all Poles are Christian. Therefore, most of Poland's important holidays are Christian holidays.

Poles celebrate Carnival from New Year's Day to Ash Wednesday, which is the beginning of Lent, a 40-day period of fasting. Young adults typically celebrate Carnival at discos and pubs, while families and older folk throw home parties. Polish elite often attend Viennese-style balls, which have dance shows and live music. Feasting reaches its peak during the last week of Carnival, from Tłusty Czwartek, or "Fat Thursday," to Ostatki, or Shrove Tuesday (literally, "lasts").

At the end of Lent comes Holy Week and Easter. In Poland, Holy Week and Easter equal Christmas in importance. Easter Sunday begins with Mass and continues with all-day feasting.

The Christmas season begins with Saint Nicholas Day on December 6. On this day, an adult dresses as the long-ago bishop. He leaves gifts for good children and sticks for naughty ones. On Wigilia, (literally, "eve") which is Christmas Eve, or December 24, Poles enjoy a

ŚMIGUS DYNGUS

Śmigus Dyngus, or "Wet Monday," is the Monday after Easter. The holiday has roots in the Christian rite of baptism, but in modern times, it has developed into a mischievous holiday for young people. Girls and boys lurk about, ready to drench unsuspecting friends or random passersby with water balloons or buckets of water. Many people live in apartment buildings, so high balconies and windows are favorite spots for ambush.

12-course meal before attending a midnight mass. They spend the next day, Christmas Day, with family, feasting and exchanging gifts.

Another celebration, All Saints' Day and All Souls' Day, which takes place on November 1 through 2, gives Poles the opportunity to remember the dead. The first day is a national holiday. The second day is dedicated to praying for the dead. People visit cemeteries, clean graves, light candles, and leave flowers to honor the departed.

Nonreligious holidays are celebrated in Poland as well. These holidays include Labor Day on May 1, Flag Day on May 2, Constitution Day on May 3, and Victory Day on May 9, which celebrates the end of World War II. Official ceremonies and parades take place to celebrate these patriotic holidays, but most Poles use them as a spring break and take off on vacation.

SPORTS

Many recreational activities thrive in Poland, from spectator to team to individual sports. Soccer, called football in Poland, is the country's most popular sport to watch and play. Poland and Ukraine together hosted the Union of European Football Associations (UEFA) European Football Championship in June and July of 2012. Other popular competitive sports include volleyball, track and field, swimming, basketball, boxing, ski jumping, handball, ice hockey, weight lifting, fencing, table tennis, and martial arts.

Thousands of fans turned out to support the Polish national soccer team during the Euro 2012 championship in Warsaw.

Poland's participation in the Olympics dates back to 1924. In 2012, 221 Polish athletes competed at the summer games in London in a variety of events. Poland took home a total of ten medals that year, including two gold medals: one in athletics and one in weight lifting.

Poles also make the most of their country's natural beauty by participating avidly in outdoor recreation. The mountains attract droves of skiers, hikers, and mountain bikers. Meanwhile, the lakes region and the Baltic Sea provide ideal venues for fishing, canoeing, kayaking, and sailing.

CHAPTER 7
POLITICS: GROWING PAINS

On April 10, 2010, an airplane carrying dozens of Polish government and military officials, including the president, prepared to land at Smolensk Air Base in Russia. The officials were headed to a memorial ceremony marking the seventieth anniversary of the Katyń massacre. In April 1940, in Russia's Katyń Forest and elsewhere, Soviet secret police executed approximately 22,000 Polish military officers, police officers, and intellectuals. Polish-Russian relations were chilly ever since, but they have been gradually improving.

The Polish airplane crashed, killing all 96 people on board. Poland found itself in a precarious position. In one fell swoop, a large number of the nation's highest-ranking public officials, including the president and

> **Due to the 1940 massacre and the 2010 plane crash, Poles refer to the Katyń Forest as "that cursed place."**

Mourners gathered to watch President Lech Kaczyński's coffin pass during a military and religious procession on April 17, 2010.

First Lady, leaders of several parties, a number of members of parliament, and many leading generals of the armed forces, had died. Suspicions, accusations, and musings swirled, straining the fragile relationship between Poland and Russia, as well as Poland's political system. Poles faced the large task of mending their shattered government, healing their grief and anger, and moving forward amid the destruction and chaos.

STABILITY OUT OF CHAOS

Since the fall of communism in 1989, Poland's government has seen many ups and downs. Lech Wałęsa, who served as the nation's first popularly elected president from the five-year term 1990 to 1995, was less skilled at leading a democratic government than he was at tearing down an undemocratic one. Fed up with infighting, chaos, and economic hardships, Poles next elected a former Communist, Aleksander Kwaśniewski, as president in 1995. Although some feared a return to communism under Kwaśniewski, it did not happen. As president, Kwaśniewski cooperated with the various political factions in Poland's parliament and won a second term. However, Poles still struggled with high unemployment and poverty—problems that persisted prior to Kwaśniewski's leadership. Kwaśniewski's second term ended in 2005, and the political pendulum swung the opposite way when Poles elected conservative Lech Kaczyński. Throughout both Kwaśniewski and Kaczyński's leadership, bickering among political factions ensued, and many young Poles felt alienated by the government's conservative and nationalistic policies.

Poland elected Bronisław Komorowski as president in 2010.

At the time of the government plane crash in 2010, neither the government nor the Polish people were in harmony. Kaczyński, who was in year five of his presidential term, was not a universally loved leader. Despite these issues, Poles came together to mourn and rebuild their government. They elected Bronisław Komorowski—a more moderate politician—as their new president, over the dead president's identical twin brother, who had briefly served as prime minister in 2006. Komorowski and Donald Tusk, who became prime minister in 2007, were still Poland's leaders in 2012.

Despite some dissention and setbacks, political experts around the world have widely praised Poland for its successful transformation since 1989. Changing from a tightly controlled Communist political and economic system to a free-market economy and a democratic government is a difficult task. Poland has managed it well, emerging with a more stable government and a stronger economy than most of its former-Communist neighbors in Central and Eastern Europe.

POLAND'S CONSTITUTION

The following lines are excerpted from the introduction to Poland's Constitution:

> Having regard for the existence and future of our Homeland,
>
> Which recovered, in 1989, the possibility of a sovereign and democratic determination of its fate,
>
> We, the Polish Nation—all citizens of the Republic . . .
>
> We call upon all those who will apply this Constitution for the good of the Third Republic to do so paying respect to the inherent dignity of the person, his or her right to freedom, the obligation of solidarity with others, and respect for these principles as the unshakeable foundation of the Republic of Poland.[1]

POLITICAL SYSTEM

Poland's government operates according to the constitution of 1997. This document describes and guarantees a wide variety of individual rights and freedoms. It also outlines the structure, methods, and relationships among the national government's key bodies and positions.

Poland's president leads the executive branch of government. The president, elected by popular vote, serves a five-year term. He or she is head of state and guarantees continuity of government, ensuring the constitution is followed and providing for national security as commander-in-chief of the military. The president calls parliamentary elections and can call for national referendums to decide important matters. The president also appoints the prime minister. The prime minister leads the cabinet, or council of ministers. The cabinet ministers are the heads of key executive departments, such as the Ministry of Environment and the Ministry of Finance.

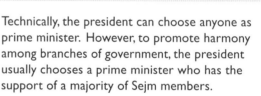

CHOOSING A PRIME MINISTER

Technically, the president can choose anyone as prime minister. However, to promote harmony among branches of government, the president usually chooses a prime minister who has the support of a majority of Sejm members.

Poland's parliament is the legislative branch of government. The parliament consists of two chambers. The lower house is called the Sejm. Its 460 members are elected by a complex system of proportional representation. Political parties win seats according to the total votes for

their candidates in a constituency. The upper house is called the Senate. Its 100 members are elected by popular vote according to province. All parliament members serve four-year terms.

STRUCTURE OF THE GOVERNMENT OF POLAND

Executive Branch	Legislative Branch	Judicial Branch
President Prime Minister Council of Ministers	Sejm Senate	Supreme Court General, Military, and Administrative Courts Constitutional Tribunal and State Tribunal

After the fall of communism, Poland's political parties were initially sharply divided between groups that emerged from Solidarity and groups that emerged post-1989. In modern Poland, this divide no longer exists. Polish political parties, similar to parties elsewhere in Europe, represent a broad range of philosophies, including social-democratic, liberal, conservative, national, rural-interest, and populist. Pundits have tried to

Poland's Sejm building in Warsaw, where the lower house meets

classify the parties as left wing, right wing, and center, but such categories do not fit well. Poland's biggest political parties are the Civic Platform (PO), the Law and Justice Party (PiS), Palikot's Movement (RP), the Polish Peasants' Party (PSL), and the Democratic Left Alliance (SLD).

Poland's judicial branch of government operates independently from the executive and legislative branches. General courts decide matters of civil, criminal, family, and labor law. Military courts deal with matters of military law. Administrative courts handle decisions about corporations and government agencies. The State Tribunal investigates elected officials' wrongdoings. The Supreme Court is the land's highest court. It is the court of last resort in appealing lower court judgments. It also clarifies laws. The president appoints Supreme Court judges for indefinite terms. The Constitutional Tribunal ensures the other branches of government adhere to the constitution and law of the land. Constitutional judges are chosen by the Sejm and serve nine-year terms.

The Supreme Court in Poland has 12 appointed judges.

The Polish flag

CHAPTER 8

ECONOMICS: A SUCCESSFUL TRANSITION

Poland has spent the past couple decades recovering from the economic decay left by communism. In 1989, despite ongoing tight governmental control, the economy was completely dysfunctional. People could not acquire many basic consumer goods, and inflation raged. The average annual inflation rate from 1990 to 2010 was 11 percent, an unhealthy rate.[1] Unemployment was low, but much of the labor force worked in government-owned industries that were sinking fast. Both industry and agriculture were technologically backward and inefficient. But the government could not afford to support—much less improve—them, and it could not get help from foreign investors because it already had a staggering foreign debt.

The government has helped rebuild Poland's economy.

Throughout the 1990s, the leaders of democratic Poland made big changes, including loosening the government's grip, to improve its economy. It privatized most businesses and let market forces, or supply and demand of goods and services, dictate prices and weed out unsustainable enterprises. Inflation eased, and the economy stabilized. Foreign investors restructured Poland's debt and provided new loans to help Poland develop its economy and increase its standard of living. The population in Poland below the international poverty line of $1.25 per day in earnings was 0 percent from 2000 to 2009.[2]

While Poland's economy still has a few weak areas, it is now quite strong overall. It has weathered the worldwide economic downturn that began in 2008 better than all the other EU nations. In fact, Poland's gross domestic product (GDP), the total value of goods and services produced inside Poland, grew nearly 16 percent from 2008 to 2011.[3] Poland's economy continues to grow steadily, and it has tax-free access to the markets of other EU nations. As a result, it has a large domestic market and is politically stable. Foreign companies and investors are eager to do business in Poland.

ECONOMIC MAKEUP

Poland's key natural resources are coal, sulfur, copper, natural gas, oil, silver, zinc, lead, salt, amber, timber, and arable land. Coal is the most abundant—and the most important—of these. Poland is the EU's

A coal miner monitors a drill in the Krupiński coal mine.

WIELICZKA SALT MINE

The Wieliczka Salt Mine near Kraków is one of Poland's most visited tourist sites. This fascinating display of Polish history, culture, and economy was named a UNESCO World Heritage Site in 1978.

Workers dug the mine's first underground shaft in the late thirteenth century. Since then, miners have excavated more than 186 miles (300 km) of tunnels 1,073 feet (327 m) deep through the rock salt. As they worked, they created complex and beautiful carvings, including many statues and three chapels. The mine is not just a tourist site, however. It has been mined continuously for seven centuries.

top coal producer, the world's ninth-largest coal producer, and the world's tenth-biggest coal user.[4] Coal burning generates 92 percent of the electricity and 89 percent of the heat used in Poland.[5]

Although coal is very important, it does not make up a huge portion of Poland's economy outside of energy production. In fact, industry overall, which includes mining, energy, and manufacturing, accounts for only 33.6 percent of the GDP and 29.2 percent of employment.[6] Poland's key industries are machine building, iron, steel, coal mining, chemicals, shipbuilding, glass making, textiles and food and beverage processing.

Poland's largest economic sector is services. This sector includes all business activity that provides useful labor instead of material goods, such as banking, transportation, retail, business services, telecommunications, hospitality services, tourism, construction, and government services.

Shoppers examine wares in Kraków. Retail makes up a large part of the Polish service industry.

Services account for approximately 63 percent of Poland's GDP and 53.4 percent of employment.[7] According to the *Warsaw Business Journal*, "Poland's services sector is driving the economy, with the automotive, gastronomic, and hairdressing sectors faring particularly well" by growing rapidly in recent years.[8] Tourism makes up another large portion of the service economy. The number of visitors to Poland has increased steadily since it joined the EU in 2004.

Poland's agricultural industry includes farming, fishing, and forestry. Polish farming is inefficient, however. Although the industry employs approximately 17.4 percent of Polish workers, it contributes only approximately 3.4 percent of the nation's GDP.[9] Poland's key agricultural products are potatoes, fruits, vegetables, wheat, poultry, eggs, pork, and dairy. Polish farmers are modernizing their methods so Poland can become more productive and profitable and import less food from other countries.

SMALL FARMS

Flying eastward into Poland, a traveler looking out the airplane window can see a gradual change in the landscape, as vast German fields fade into much tinier Polish farms. Approximately 88 percent of Polish farmers produce food mostly for their own households. Their farms are small—usually 12.4 acres (5 ha) or less. The remaining 12 percent of farmers have larger farms—typically more than 37 acres (15 ha), but a small percentage ranges up to 494 acres (200 ha)—and produce 90 percent of Poland's agricultural output.[11]

Poland's foreign trade is relatively well balanced. The country exported approximately $194 billion and imported approximately $208 billion worth of goods in 2011.[10] Poland's main exports are cars, machinery, furniture, and iron and steel products. Another export is

In Poland, farmers often produce food for their own families rather than on an industrial scale.

Bolesławiec pottery, named
after the town where it is
created. The pottery is a
distinct type of handcrafted,
hand-painted stoneware.
Poland's main export
partners are Germany,
France, the United Kingdom,
the Czech Republic,
Netherlands, and Russia.

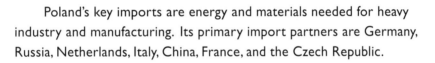

POLISH CURRENCY

Polish banknotes come in denominations
of 10, 20, 50, 100, and 200 złotych. Coins come
in denominations of 1, 2, 5, 10, 20, and 50 groszy,
and 1, 2, and 5 złotych. One złoty equals 100 groszy.
Approximately 3.3 złotych equal US$1.[13]

Poland's key imports are energy and materials needed for heavy
industry and manufacturing. Its primary import partners are Germany,
Russia, Netherlands, Italy, China, France, and the Czech Republic.

INFRASTRUCTURE

Both the transportation infrastructure and communication infrastructure
in Poland have improved dramatically since 1989 and continue to do
so. Development has happened quickly since Poland joined the EU in
2004 and began investing large amounts of money into modernization.

Poland ranks fifteenth in the world in both its roadway and
railway networks.[12] It has 183,526 miles (295,356 km) of paved roads
and 79,934 miles (128,641 km) of unpaved roads. It has 12,072 miles

Polish currency

A freight train carrying coal navigates one of Poland's many railways.

(19,428 km) of railways.[14] Poland is a key country through which EU imports and exports must pass, so it is important the country keeps expanding its roadways and railways. It is also important Poland's transportation networks are extensive and well maintained.

Poland's air infrastructure and water infrastructure are somewhat less developed but are also improving. The nation currently has 125 airports, including 86 with paved runways.[15] Warsaw Chopin Airport is the main hub for LOT Polish Airlines. Poland is also home to 2,484 miles (3,997 km) of navigable rivers and canals and four major seaports: Gdańsk, Gdynia, Świnoujście, and Szczecin. Year-round passenger ferries link Poland with other Baltic countries.

Poland has a fully modern telecommunications network. Poles have 9.5 million landline telephones, 46 million cellular phones, and 22.5 million Internet users.[16]

Polish media is vibrant, diverse, and largely independent. Government-owned Polish Television (TVP) and its four channels are a major source of information for most citizens. The constitution forbids censorship and guarantees freedom of the press. Print media and radio are mostly privately owned.

LOOKING FORWARD

Poland has regained strength economically since communism, and it is in position to continue developing its economy in order to remain competitive within and outside the EU. For example, the average labor force participation rate for countries in the EU is 77.4 percent. Poland's rate is 66.5 percent.[17] The population of Polish migrant workers immigrating to Western European

> **The Polish government plans to connect all major cities with a high-speed rail network by 2020.**

ECONOMIC GROUPS

Poland belongs to three key international economic organizations. The European Union (EU) is a partnership of 27 member nations.[19] Poland joined in 2004. Its purpose is to help people, goods, services, and money move freely between its member nations. EU members belong to a single economic market and have open borders. Most use the euro as currency, but Poland uses the złoty.

Poland also belongs to the Organization for Economic Cooperation and Development (OECD). The OECD is an alliance of 34 member nations.[20] Poland joined in 1996. The organization's mission is to promote policies that improve the economic and social well-being of all people.

In 1995, Poland became a member of the World Trade Organization (WTO). The WTO is a global association that helps its 157 member nations trade with one another.[21] It provides a venue for establishing rules, negotiating agreements, and settling disputes.

countries, especially the United Kingdom, rose recently. As of 2011, hundreds of thousands of Poles lived in the United Kingdom.[18] If Polish businesses can find a way to employ more able-bodied adults, they can increase the nation's productivity.

Privatization is another ongoing and important goal. The government still owns many large enterprises, especially in transportation, mining, chemicals, energy, finance, and defense. Economists believe privatization of these industries is the last big, unfinished task of Poland's transformation from communism to capitalism.

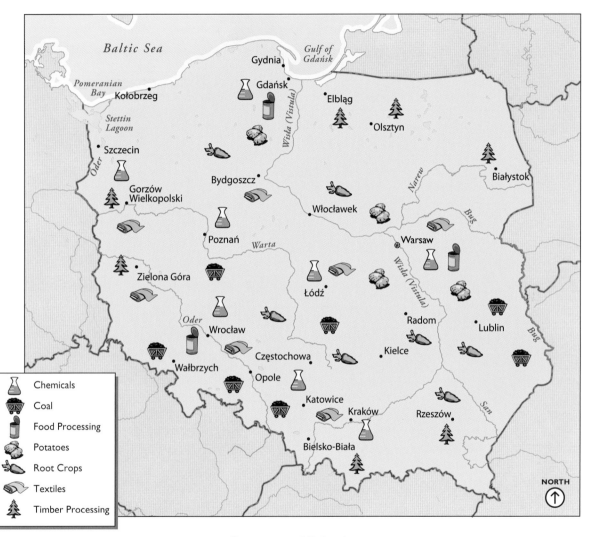

Resources of Poland

Baltic Sea

Gulf of Gdańsk

Pomeranian Bay

Stettin Lagoon

Gydnia

Gdańsk

Kołobrzeg

Elbląg

Olsztyn

Szczecin

Gorzów Wielkopolski

Bydgoszcz

Białystok

Włocławek

Poznań

Warsaw

Zielona Góra

Łódź

Wrocław

Radom

Lublin

Wałbrzych

Częstochowa

Kielce

Opole

Katowice

Kraków

Rzeszów

Bielsko-Biała

Oder

Wisła (Vistula)

Narew

Bug

Warta

San

NORTH

Chemicals
Coal
Food Processing
Potatoes
Root Crops
Textiles
Timber Processing

CHAPTER 9
POLAND TODAY

Poland today is a much different place than it was 30—or even 20—years ago. As the government and the economy have changed, so has Polish society.

THE ATTITUDE GAP

What Poles think of the many changes to their way of life in modern Poland depends largely on how old they are and where they live. Older citizens have lived through a great deal of change. They may remember the horror and heroism of World War II. They have lived many years of their lives under communism. Chances are they have never had much material wealth and have learned to value family, faith, and tradition intensely. Older Poles tend to think and behave conservatively. They have mixed feelings about modern

"A guest in the house is God in the house."
—Polish proverb

Elder Poles have a different perspective than youth, as political, economic, and social issues have shifted dramatically between the generations.

Polish society. They are proud of their nation's accomplishments, and they enjoy having so many choices. They can buy, say, and do things that were once unthinkable. But many members of the older generation are concerned about the country's youth, who often seem obsessed with success and unmoored from the cultural anchors that have helped Poles survive political, economic, and social shifts throughout history.

Younger adults and teenagers in Poland have a very different perspective. They may remember communism, but their memories are from their childhood. Much of the Polish youth have lived most—or all—of their lives under a democratically elected government and in a free-market economy. They embrace opportunities to learn, achieve, and acquire. Many are ambitious to improve their educational or professional status, have a full array of modern conveniences, and follow the latest fashions. Young Poles tend to be pragmatic and open-minded.

Location plays a role in today's Polish ideologies as well. Economic and social opportunities are plentiful in Poland's cities, but it is difficult to scrape by in the countryside. As a result, urban dwellers tend to be

FRUSTRATED IN FAITH

Although a large portion of young Poles cherish their Catholic beliefs, some are turning away from the Catholic Church as an institution. They are frustrated with the Church's unwillingness to discuss modern issues such as contraception and abortion. Many are also disappointed with its failure to address other current controversial issues, such as the HIV/AIDS crisis.

Poles typically have close relationships with extended family and spend time together socially.

more ambitious and more liberal, while farmers and other rural dwellers tend to be less ambitious and more conservative.

HOME AND FAMILY

Despite the attitude gap, family is important to everyone in Poland. Most young Poles aspire to marry and have children. Extended families

A Polish *dziadek*, or grandfather, aids his grandson in church.

spend a great deal of time together. Retired grandparents often live with their married offspring and help care for the home and children. Polish parents and grandparents vigilantly protect and lavishly dote upon their children and grandchildren. This caregiving lasts until the early teens, when parents give their children much more freedom. Polish teens become adults when they turn 18. At this age, they can vote and can drink alcohol legally.

In Poland, the home is more than just a residence. It is a social meeting place that is always open to relatives, friends, and guests. Most Poles live in apartment buildings. They usually own—not rent—their apartments, and they invest a large amount of money and effort into making their homes as pleasant and comfortable as possible. Many apartment buildings in Polish cities are relics from Communist rule. The government also created garden allotments in large cities with dense apartment populations. These gardens were meant to create a place workers could tend for relaxation. Many of these gardens still exist today, and can be leased by residents for recreational gardening or growing food.

EDUCATION

Polish culture places great value on education, and Poland has a well-developed education system. The law previously required children to attend school from age seven until 18, but it will change in 2013 to beginning a year earlier, at age six.[1] These factors lead to a high literacy rate. Nearly 100 percent—99.5 percent to be exact—of the Polish population over age 15 can read and write.[2]

Children begin primary school when they are seven years of age and attend for six years. At the end of the sixth year, students must take a comprehensive exam. After passing the exam, students begin secondary school.

The exam Polish students must pass at the end of high school is called the *matura* exam.

Secondary school includes gymnasium and high school. Gymnasium lasts for three years. At the end of the third year, students take an exam and then move on to high school. This includes two- to three-year basic vocational schools, three-year general secondary schools, three-year specialized secondary schools, and four-year technical secondary schools. Students choose which type of school to attend based on their interests and future career paths. A vocational school is called a *zawodówka*, and a nonvocational school is a *liceum*. At the end of high school, students must pass an exam. Then students may begin the careers for

Students in class at a school in Gdańsk

EDUCATION STATISTICS

Primary School	Secondary School	Higher Education
96 percent enrolled (2007–2010)[3]	93 percent enrolled (2007–2010)[4]	36.8 percent enrolled (ages 19–24, 2004–2005)[5]

which they have trained or go on to higher education. Higher education in Poland is available at dozens of public and private universities and specialized institutes.

FACING THE FUTURE

As today's young Poles become adults, they face both great opportunity and great responsibility. Past generations have ensured Poland's survival through centuries of hardship. They have brought freedom and prosperity to the nation. Poland's future is brighter than it has been for centuries.

It will take a great deal of hard work to keep Poland's future bright. Poland can thrive if young Poles continue the work of cleaning

A group of young Poles represented their nation at World Youth Day in Germany in 2005.

"Gotowe zdrowie, kto chorobę powie."
—Polish proverb meaning sharing problems lessens them

up Poland's land, air, and water and finding a sustainable way to use their nation's remaining natural resources. Completing Poland's economic transition will also provide improved stability. Poland has learned from hard political lessons. Throughout these challenges and changes, Poles continue working together for the common good.

Poland's youth face a bright future built upon the nation's collective knowledge, growth, and determination to overcome many challenges.

[TIMELINE]

800,000 BCE	People begin living in the area that is now Poland.
730s BCE	People build the Lusatian settlement of Biskupin near the modern town of Żnin.
ca. 500 CE	The Slavs move into Poland from the east.
963	Mieszko I of the Piast dynasty becomes the first king of Poland.
966	Mieszko I unites the Slavic tribes of Poland and accepts Christianity on their behalf, forming the kingdom of Poland.
1385	The leaders of Poland and Lithuania join forces in the Union of Krewo, forming the kingdom of Poland-Lithuania.
1490s	Polish scholar Nicolaus Copernicus revolutionizes the field of astronomy with his observations and conclusions.
1573	Members of Polish Sejm pass the Warsaw Confederation, which guarantees freedom of religious practice for all.
1772–1795	Prussia, Austria, and Russia divide and lay claim to areas of Poland three times, wiping Poland off the European map.
1914–1918	World War I takes place. Poland is a key battleground, and more than 1 million Poles die. Poland regains independence at war's end.
1920	Marshal Józef Piłsudski and Polish forces defeat the Soviet army at the Battle of Warsaw, preserving Poland's independence.
1926	Piłsudski overturns Poland's democratically elected government in a military coup.

1933	Adolf Hitler rises to power in Germany.
1939–1945	World War II takes place. The Soviet Union and Nazi Germany occupy Poland. Approximately 6 million Polish citizens die.
1945	Poland falls into the Soviet sphere of influence. With Soviet support, Communists win control of the Polish government.
1978	Polish cardinal Karol Wojtyła becomes Pope John Paul II.
1980	Shipyard workers in Gdańsk go on strike. They form the Solidarity trade union.
1981–1983	Communist authorities impose military law in Poland.
1989	In August, a new government begins replacing the Communist system with a democracy and a free-market economy.
1997	Poland adopts its current constitution.
1999	Poland joins NATO.
2004	Poland joins the EU.
2010	On April 10, Poland's president, Lech Kaczyński, and 95 other Poles die in a plane crash near Smolensk, Russia.
2012	Poland and Ukraine together host the UEFA European Football Championship.

FACTS AT YOUR FINGERTIPS

GEOGRAPHY

Official name: Republic of Poland (in Polish, Rzeczpospolita Polska)

Area: 120,728 square miles (312,685 sq km)

Climate: Continental, with generally warm, moderate summers and cold, snowy winters

Highest elevation: Mount Rysy, 8,199 feet (2,499 m) above sea level

Lowest elevation: Raczki Elbląskie, 6.6 feet (2 m) below sea level

Significant geographic features: Tatra Mountains; Wisła River

PEOPLE

Population (July 2012 est.): 38,415,284

Most populous city: Warsaw

Ethnic groups: Ethnic Poles, 96.7 percent; Germans, 0.4 percent; Belarusians, 0.1 percent; Ukrainians, 0.1 percent; other, 2.7 percent

Percentage of residents living in urban areas: 61 percent

Life expectancy: 76 years at birth (world rank: 77)

Language(s): Polish

Religion(s): Roman Catholicism, 89.8 percent; Eastern Orthodox Christianity, 1.3 percent; Protestantism, 0.3 percent; unspecified, 8.6 percent

GOVERNMENT AND ECONOMY

Government: republic

Capital: Warsaw

Date of adoption of current constitution: April 2, 1997

Head of state: president

Head of government: prime minister

Legislature: parliament, consists of the Sejm and the Senate

Currency: złoty

Industries and natural resources: Poland's main natural resources are coal, sulfur, copper, natural gas, oil, silver, zinc, lead, salt, amber, and arable land. Its key industries are machine building, iron and steel, coal mining, chemicals, shipbuilding, food and beverage processing, glassmaking, and textiles. Poland exports cars, machinery, furniture, and iron and steel products. It imports energy and materials needed for heavy industry and manufacturing.

NATIONAL SYMBOLS

Holidays: Labor Day on May 1, Flag Day on May 2, and Constitution Day on May 3. Poles remember the Battle of Warsaw on August 15 and celebrate their independence on November 11.

Flag: A rectangle divided into two equal horizontal bands, white above and red below

National anthem: "Jeszcze Polska Nie Zginęła" (Poland Is Not Yet Lost), also called "Dabrowski's Mazurka"

National animal: white-tailed eagle

KEY PEOPLE

Mieszko I (922–992) united the Slavic tribes of Poland and accepted Christianity on their behalf, forming the kingdom of Poland.

Kazimierz III (1310–1370) became known as King Kazimierz the Great because of his exceptional wisdom and skill as a ruler.

Nicolaus Copernicus (1473–1543), astronomer and mathematician, proposed a sun-centered model of the solar system that revolutionized humankind's view of the universe.

Karol Wojtyła (1920–2005) became John Paul II, the first Polish pope, and played a central role in the fall of communism in Eastern Europe.

Lech Wałęsa (1943–) led Poland's Solidarity union, won the Nobel Peace Prize, and served as Poland's first postcommunist president.

PROVINCES OF POLAND

Province; Capital

Dolnośląskie; Wrocław

Kujawsko-Pomorskie; Bydgoszcz and Toruń

Łódzkie; Łódź

Lubelskie; Lublin

Lubuskie; Gorzów Wielkopolski and Zielona Góra

Małopolskie; Kraków

Mazowieckie; Warsaw

Opolskie; Opole

Podkarpackie; Rzeszów

Podlaskie; Białystok

Pomorskie; Gdańsk

Śląskie; Katowice

Świętokrzyskie; Kielce

Warmińsko-Mazurskie; Olsztyn

Wielkopolskie; Poznań

Zachodniopomorskie; Szczecin

[GLOSSARY]

arable

Fertile and fit for agriculture.

benevolent dictator

Someone holding complete control but claiming to have the people and the nation's well-being in mind.

communism

An economic system defined by collective ownership of property and the organization of labor for common advantage; a government system in which a single party holds power and the state controls the economy.

conservative

Supporting established cultural norms and institutions.

deciduous

A type of plant or tree that sheds its leaves annually.

democracy

A government selected by the people through free elections.

dynasty

A succession of rulers from the same family or line.

exclave

A territory that belongs to another territory without sharing a border.

free-market economy

An economic system in which supply and demand of goods and services dictate prices and other economic decisions.

infrastructure

A country's transportation and communications networks.

left wing

The more liberal—less traditional—division of a group, especially of a political party.

liberal

Supporting the idea that institutions and cultural norms can change as societal attitudes shift.

monarchy

A government led by a hereditary leader who has a lifetime term, such as a king or queen.

nomadic

The seasonally traveling lifestyle of a group of people who have no fixed residence.

pagan

Ancient, pre-Christian religions that include worshipping different gods of nature or believing in spirits that inhabit natural places, beings, and things.

regime

A mode of rule or management.

right wing

The more conservative division of a group, especially of a political party.

ADDITIONAL RESOURCES

SELECTED BIBLIOGRAPHY

"At a Glance: Poland." *UNICEF*. UNICEF, n.d. Web. 12 Oct. 2012.

Bureau of European and Eurasian Affairs. "Background Note: Poland." *US Department of State*. US State Department, 22 Mar. 2012. Web. 12 Oct. 2012.

Curtis, Glenn E., ed. *Poland: A Country Study*. 3rd ed. Washington, DC: Federal Research Division, Library of Congress, 1994. *Library of Congress: Researchers*. Web. 12 Oct. 2012.

"The World Factbook: Poland." *Central Intelligence Agency*. Central Intelligence Agency, 4 Oct. 2012. Web. 12 Oct. 2012.

FURTHER READINGS

Baker, Mark, and Kit F. Chung. *Frommer's Poland*. 2nd ed. Mississauga, ON: Wiley, 2011. Print.

Kelly, Eric P. *The Trumpeter of Kraków*. 1929. New York: Simon, 1992. Print.

Lobel, Anita. *No Pretty Pictures*. New York: Greenwillow, 2008. Print.

WEB LINKS

To learn more about Poland, visit ABDO Publishing Company online at **www.abdopublishing.com**. Web sites about Poland are featured on our Book Links page. These links are routinely monitored and updated to provide the most current information available.

PLACES TO VISIT

If you are ever in Poland, consider checking out these important and interesting sites!

Auschwitz-Birkenau Memorial and Museum

This sobering site includes the Auschwitz I concentration camp and the Auschwitz II–Birkenau extermination camp established by the Nazis during World War II. Its goals are to honor the camps' victims, educate the public, and conduct research on the Holocaust.

Monastery of Jasna Góra

Jasna Góra, in the city of Częstochowa, is the spiritual capital of Poland. It is home to the shrine of the *Black Madonna*.

Wawel Hill

Wawel Hill, a limestone cliff overlooking the Wisła River at the southern tip of Kraków's Old Town, is the birthplace and erstwhile capital of Poland. The sprawling complex includes a cathedral, castle, armory, residences, fortifications, gardens, tombs, caves, and ruins.

Zakopane

This resort town in Poland's Tatras Mountains is famous for its winter sports, arts scene, and picturesque architecture.

SOURCE NOTES

CHAPTER 1. A VISIT TO POLAND
1. Glenn E. Curtis, ed. *Poland: A Country Study*. 3rd ed. Washington, DC: Federal Research Division, Library of Congress, 1994. *Library of Congress: Researchers*. Web. 12 Oct. 2012.

CHAPTER 2. GEOGRAPHY: LAND OF PLAINS
1. "Climate." *Polska: Official Promotional Website of the Republic of Poland*. Ministry of Foreign Affairs, n.d. Web. 12 Oct. 2012.

2. Glenn E. Curtis, ed. *Poland: A Country Study*. 3rd ed. Washington, DC: Federal Research Division, Library of Congress, 1994. *Library of Congress: Researchers*. Web. 12 Oct. 2012.

3. "Lodz, Poland." *Weatherbase*. Canty and Associates, 2012. Web. 12 Oct. 2012.

4. "Poland." *Weatherbase*. Canty and Associates, 2012. Web. 12 Oct. 2012.

CHAPTER 3. ANIMALS AND NATURE: PROGRESS AND PRESERVATION
1. "Poland Information." *Poland.ph*. Poland.ph, n.d. Web. 12 Oct. 2012.

2. "Summary Statistics: Summaries by Country, Table 5, Threatened Species in Each Country." *IUCN Red List of Threatened Species*. International Union for Conservation of Nature and Natural Resources, 2011. Web. 12 Oct. 2012.

3. Matt Walker. "European Bison on 'Genetic Brink.'" *BBC: Earth News*. BBC, 4 Aug. 2009. Web. 12 Oct. 2012.

4. "Birds of the Białowieża Forest." *Laboratory of Forest Biology: Wrocław University*. Laboratory of Forest Biology: Wrocław University, 2012. Web. 12 Oct. 2012.

5. *Polish National Parks*. Ministry of the Environment, 20 Apr. 2008. Web. 12 Oct. 2012.

CHAPTER 4. HISTORY: POLAND'S PERSEVERANCE
1. Glenn E. Curtis, ed. *Poland: A Country Study*. 3rd ed. Washington, DC: Federal Research Division, Library of Congress, 1994. *Library of Congress: Researchers*. Web. 12 Oct. 2012.

2. Ibid.

3. Tadeusz Piotrowski. *Poland's Holocaust: Ethnic Strife, Collaboration with Occupying Forces and Genocide in the Second Republic, 1918–1947*. Jefferson, NC: McFarland, 1998. *Google Book Search*. Web. 12 Oct. 2012.

4. Glenn E. Curtis, ed. *Poland: A Country Study*. 3rd ed. Washington, DC: Federal Research Division, Library of Congress, 1994. *Library of Congress: Researchers*. Web. 12 Oct. 2012.

5. Ibid.

6. Ibid.

7. "The Nobel Peace Prize 1983: Lech Walesa." *Nobelprize.org: The Official Web Site of the Nobel Prize.* Nobel Media, 5 Oct. 1983. Web. 12 Oct. 2012.

8. Cal Thomas. "Pope Strengthened Church, Weakened Communism." *Baltimore Sun.* Baltimore Sun, 6 Apr. 2005. Web. 12 Oct. 2012.

9. Stephen White. *Communism and Its Collapse.* London; New York: Routledge, 2001. *Google Book Search.* Web. 12 Oct. 2012.

CHAPTER 5. PEOPLE: SHARED ROOTS

1. James Mayfield. "Ethnic and Religious Map of Poland Before the Nazi Invasion." *European Heritage Library.* European Heritage Library, n.d. Web. 12 Oct. 2012.

2. "The World Factbook: Poland." *Central Intelligence Agency.* Central Intelligence Agency, 4 Oct. 2012. Web. 12 Oct. 2012.

3. "Situation of Roma in Poland." *V4: Mayors for Roma Inclusion Forum.* International Visegrad Fund, n.d. Web. 12 Oct. 2012.

4. "The World Factbook: Poland." *Central Intelligence Agency.* Central Intelligence Agency, 4 Oct. 2012. Web. 12 Oct. 2012.

5. Ibid.

6. Glenn E. Curtis, ed. *Poland: A Country Study.* 3rd ed. Washington, DC: Federal Research Division, Library of Congress, 1994. *Library of Congress: Researchers.* Web. 12 Oct. 2012.

7. "The World Factbook: Poland." *Central Intelligence Agency.* Central Intelligence Agency, 4 Oct. 2012. Web. 12 Oct. 2012.

8. Ibid.

9. M. Paul Lewis, ed. "Languages of Poland." *Ethnologue: Languages of the World.* SIL International, n.d. Web. 12 Oct. 2012.

10. James Mayfield. "Ethnic and Religious Map of Poland Before the Nazi Invasion." *European Heritage Library.* European Heritage Library, n.d. Web. 12 Oct. 2012.

11. "The World Factbook: Poland." *Central Intelligence Agency.* Central Intelligence Agency, 4 Oct. 2012. Web. 12 Oct. 2012.

12. "Global Christianity." *Pew Forum on Religion and Public Life.* Pew Forum on Religion and Public Life, 19 Dec. 2011. Web. 12 Oct. 2012.

13. Michael P. Duricy. "Black Madonnas: Our Lady of Czestochowa." *The Mary Page.*

SOURCE NOTES CONTINUED

University of Dayton: The Marian Library/International Marian Research Institute, 26 Mar. 2008. Web. 12 Oct. 2012.

CHAPTER 6. CULTURE: PROUDLY POLISH

1. "Henryk Sienkiewicz 1846–1916." *Polish American Cultural Center*. Polish American Cultural Center, n.d. Web. 12 Oct. 2012.

2. Nobel Foundation. "The Nobel Prize in Literature 1978: Isaac Bashevis Singer." *Nobelprize.org*. Nobel Media, n.d. Web. 12 Oct. 2012.

3. Chris Borowski and Andrew Heavens, ed. "Polish Nobel Winning Poet Szymborska Dies at 88." *Reuters*. Thomson Reuters, 1 Feb. 2012. Web. 12 Oct. 2012.

4. "Poland Nobel Poetry Laureate Wislawa Szymborska Dies." *BBC News Europe*. BBC, 1 Feb. 2012. Web. 12 Oct. 2012.

5. Chris Borowski and Andrew Heavens, ed. "Polish Nobel Winning Poet Szymborska Dies at 88." *Reuters*. Thomson Reuters, 1 Feb. 2012. Web. 12 Oct. 2012.

CHAPTER 7. POLITICS: GROWING PAINS

1. "The Constitution of the Republic of Poland of 2nd April, 1997." *Sejm: Rzeczypospolitej Polskiej*. Kancelaria Semju, 2 Apr. 1997. Web. 12 Oct. 2012.

CHAPTER 8. ECONOMICS: A SUCCESSFUL TRANSITION

1. "At a Glance: Poland." *UNICEF*. UNICEF, n.d. Web. 12 Oct. 2012.

2. Ibid.

3. Bureau of European and Eurasian Affairs. "Background Note: Poland." *US Department of State*. US State Department, 22 Mar. 2012. Web. 12 Oct. 2012.

4. "Coal Profile: Poland." *World Coal Association*. World Coal Association, Aug. 2011. Web. 12 Oct. 2012.

5. Ibid.

6. "The World Factbook: Poland." *Central Intelligence Agency*. Central Intelligence Agency, 4 Oct. 2012. Web. 12 Oct. 2012.

7. Ibid.

8. "Services Sector Drives Polish Economy." *Warsaw Business Journal*. Valkea Media, 2011. Web. 12 Oct. 2012.

9. "The World Factbook: Poland." *Central Intelligence Agency*. Central Intelligence Agency, 4 Oct. 2012. Web. 12 Oct. 2012.

10. Ibid.

11. Bureau of European and Eurasian Affairs. "Background Note: Poland." *US Department of State*. US State Department, 22 Mar. 2012. Web. 12 Oct. 2012.

12. "The World Factbook: Poland." *Central Intelligence Agency*. Central Intelligence Agency, 4 Oct. 2012. Web. 12 Oct. 2012.

13. "Polish Zloty (PLN) and United States Dollar (USD) Currency Exchange Rate Conversion Calculator." *CoinMill.com: The Currency Convertor*. Stephen Ostermiller, 15 Oct. 2012. Web. 15 Oct. 2012.

14. "The World Factbook: Poland." *Central Intelligence Agency*. Central Intelligence Agency, 4 Oct. 2012. Web. 12 Oct. 2012.

15. Ibid.

16. Ibid.

17. Bureau of European and Eurasian Affairs. "Background Note: Poland." *US Department of State*. US State Department, 22 Mar. 2012. Web. 12 Oct. 2012.

18. Alan Travis. "Migration to UK Rises by 21% Despite Coalition Clampdown." *Guardian*. Guardian News and Media, 25 Aug. 2011. Web. 15 Oct. 2012.

19. "Countries." *Europa.eu: European Union*. n.p., n.d. Web. 15 Oct. 2012.

20. "Members and Partners: Current Membership." *OECD*. OECD, n.d. Web. 15 Oct. 2012.

21. "The WTO." *World Trade Organization*. World Trade Organization, 2012. Web. 15 Oct. 2012.

CHAPTER 9. POLAND TODAY

1. Education, Audiovisual & Culture Executive Agency. "Organisation of the Education System in Poland: 2009/2010." *European Commission: Education, Audiovisual & Culture Executive Agency*. European Union, n.d. Web. 15 Oct. 2012.

2. "The World Factbook: Literacy." *Central Intelligence Agency*. Central Intelligence Agency, n.d. Web. 12 Oct. 2012.

3. "At a Glance: Poland." *UNICEF*. UNICEF, n.d. Web. 12 Oct. 2012.

4. Ibid.

5. Oliver Fulton, et al. "OECD Reviews of Tertiary Education: Poland." *Ministry of Science and Higher Education: Republic of Poland*. Ministry of Science and Higher Education, 2007. Web. 15 Oct. 2012.

[INDEX]

[PHOTO CREDITS]

Shutterstock Images, cover, 5 (top), 11, 29, 30, 110, 131, 133; iStockphoto/Thinkstock, 2, 14, 21, 40, 88, 102, 108, 112; Hermann J. Knippertz/AP Images, 5 (center), 124; Erhard Nerger/Getty Images, 5 (bottom), 39; Michal Kolodziejski/Shutterstock Images, 6, 130; Matt Kania/Map Hero, Inc, 9, 22, 25, 68, 115; Henry T. Keiser/Photolibrary/Getty Images, 13; Alex White/Shutterstock Images, 18; Copestello/Shutterstock Images, 26; Andrew Astbury/Shutterstock Images, 32; Falk Kienas/iStockphoto, 37; Pawel Kazmierczak/Shutterstock Images, 45; DEA Picture Library/De Agostini/Getty Images, 46; The Bridgeman Art Library/Getty Images, 49, 128 (top); World History Archive/Alamy, 51; UIG/Getty Images, 57; AP Images, 59, 61, 128 (bottom); Alik Keplicz/AP Images, 64, 82, 84; Janek Skarzynski/AFP/Getty Images, 66, 120; Lonely Planet/Getty Images, 73, 107; Mari/Vatican Pool/AP Images, 76, 129 (top); Chris Niedenthal/Time Life Pictures/Getty Images, 78; Sergey Ponomarev/AP Images, 91; Sean Gallup/Getty Images, 92, 129 (bottom); Czarek Komorowski/AP Images, 95; Luke Daniek/iStockphoto, 98; Stockbyte/Thinkstock, 101, 132; Bloomberg/Getty images, 105; Petr David Josek/AP Images, 116; David Grossman/Alamy, 119; Peter Arkell/Imagestate Media Partners Limited-Impact Photos/Alamy, 123; Tiziana Fabi/AFP/Getty Images, 127